THE PRESIDENTS

Editor

Fred L. Israel

VOLUME 3

Zachary Taylor 1849 – Ulysses S. Grant 1877

Grolier Educational

SHERMAN TURNPIKE, DANBURY, CONNECTICUT

The publisher gratefully acknowledges permission from the sources to reproduce photos that appear on the cover.

Volume 1
J. Adams – New York Historical Society
J. Monroe – Library of Congress

Volume 2
J. K. Polk; A. Jackson; J. Tyler – Library of Congress
J. Q. Adams – National Archives

Volume 3
U. S. Grant – National Archives
A. Johnson; Z. Taylor – Library of Congress

Volume 4
B. Harrison; W. McKinley; J. A. Garfield – Library of Congress

Volume 5
H. Hoover; W. G. Harding – Library of Congress
T. Roosevelt – National Archives

Volume 6
D. D. Eisenhower – Library of Congress
L. B. Johnson – White House

Volume 7
B. Clinton – The White House
R. Reagan – Bush/Reagan Committee
G. Bush – Cynthia Johnson, The White House

Volume 8
T. Roosevelt – National Archives
B. Clinton – The White House

Published 1997 exclusively for the school and library market by Grolier Educational

Sherman Turnpike, Danbury, Connecticut

© 1997 by Charles E. Smith Books, Inc.

Set: ISBN 0-7172-7642-2

Volume 3: ISBN 0-7172-7645-7

Library of Congress number:

The presidents.

    p. cm.

    Contents: v. 1. 1789–1825 (Washington–Monroe) — v. 2. 1825–1849 (Adams–Polk)

    v. 3. 1849–1877 (Taylor–Grant) — v. 4. 1877–1901 (Hayes–McKinley) — v. 5.1901–1933 (T. Roosevelt–Hoover)

    v. 6. 1933–1969 (F. D. Roosevelt–L. B. Johnson) — v. 7. 1969–1997 (Nixon–Clinton)

    v. 8. Documents, suggested reading, charts, tables, appendixes

1. Presidents – United States – Juvenile literature.
[1. Presidents.]   96-31491
E176.1.P9175   1997   CIP
973.099 — dc20   AC

For information, address the publisher
Grolier Educational, Sherman Turnpike, Danbury, Connecticut 06816

Printed in the United States of America

Cover design by Smart Graphics

TABLE OF CONTENTS

VOLUME THREE

CONTRIBUTORS

EDITOR

Fred L. Israel received his Ph.D. from Columbia University. He has written several books for young adults including *Franklin D. Roosevelt, Henry Kissinger,* and *Know Your Government: The FBI.* Dr. Israel is also the editor of *History of American Presidential Elections, 1789-1968, The Chief Executive: Inaugural Addresses of the Presidents from George Washington to Lyndon Johnson,* and *The State of the Union Messages of the Presidents of the United States.* His most recent book is *Running for President, The Candidates and Their Images,* a two-volume work with Arthur M. Schlesinger, Jr. and David J. Frent.

Dr. Israel is Professor, Department of History, The City College of the City University of New York.

CONTRIBUTORS

Donald C. Bacon is a Washington-based journalist specializing in the presidency and Congress. He served as staff writer of *The Wall Street Journal* and assistant managing editor of *U.S. News and World Report.* A former Congressional Fellow, he is the author of *Rayburn: A Biography* and *Congress and You.* He is coeditor of *The Encyclopedia of the United States Congress.*

Hendrik Booraem V received his Ph.D. from The Johns Hopkins University. He taught social studies at Strom Thurmond High School, South Carolina, for many years. He has been Adjunct Professor at Rutgers University, Camden, Alvernia College, Lehigh University, and the State University of New York at Purchase. Dr. Booraem is the author of *The Formation of the Republican Party in New York: Politics and Conscience in the Antebellum North, The Road to Respectability: James A. Garfield and His World, 1844-1852,* and *The Provincial: Calvin Coolidge and His World, 1885-1895.*

Thomas Bracken received his B.A. and M.A., summa cum laude, from The City College of the City University of New York. He is currently enrolled in the doctoral program there, and he is Adjunct Professor of History.

David Burner received his Ph.D. from Columbia University. He is Professor of American History at the State University of New York at Stony Brook. Among Dr. Burner's many publications are *John F. Kennedy and a New Generation, The Torch is Passed: The Kennedy Brothers and American Liberalism* (with Thomas R. West) and *The Politics of Provincialism: The Democratic Party in Transition, 1918-1932.* He is also the coauthor of *Firsthand America: A History of the United States.*

Gary Cohn received his M.A. in Popular Culture Studies from Bowling Green State University in 1980 and has completed course work towards the doctorate in American History at the State University of New York at Stony Brook. As an Adjunct Professor he has taught history at The City College of the City University of New York and creative writing and composition at the C.W. Post campus of Long Island University.

Richard Nelson Current is University Distinguished Professor of History, Emeritus, at the University of North Carolina, Greensboro and former President of the Southern Historical Association. Among Dr. Current's many books are *Speaking of Abraham Lincoln: The Man and His Meaning for Our Times, Lincoln and the First Shot, The Lincoln Nobody Knows, Lincoln the President: Last Full Measure,* and with T. Harry Williams and Frank Freidel, *American History: A Survey.*

James B. Gardner received his Ph.D. from Vanderbilt University. He has been Deputy Executive Director of the American Historical Association since 1986 and Acting Executive Director of that organization since 1994. Dr. Gardner was with the American Association for State and Local History from 1979 to 1986, where he served in a variety of capacities, including Director of Education and Special Programs. Among his many publications is *A Historical Guide to the United States.*

Anne-Marie Grimaud received her B.A. from the Sorbonne, Paris and her M.A. from the State University of New York at Stony Brook, where she is currently enrolled in the doctoral program in American History.

Douglas Kinnard graduated from the United States Military Academy and served in Europe during World War II. He also served in Korea and Vietnam and retired as Brigadier General. He then received his Ph.D. from Princeton University. Dr. Kinnard is Professor Emeritus, University of Vermont and was Chief of Military History, U.S. Army. Among Dr. Kinnard's books are *Ike 1890–1990: A Pictorial History, President Eisenhower and Strategy Management: A Study in Defense Politics,* and *Maxwell Taylor and The American Experience in Vietnam.*

Robert A. Raber received his J.D. from the Law School, University of California, Berkeley. He retired from law practice and received his M.A. from The City College of the City University of New York, where he is enrolled in the doctoral program.

Donald A. Ritchie received his Ph.D. from the University of Maryland. Dr. Ritchie is on the Executive Committee of the American Historical Association, and he has been Associate Historian, United States Senate for 20 years. Among his many publications are *Press Gallery: Congress and the Washington Correspondents, The Young Oxford Companion to the Congress of the United States,* and *Oxford Profiles of American Journalists.*

Robert A. Rutland is Professor of History Emeritus, University of Virginia. He was editor in chief of *The Papers of James Madison* for many years, and he was coordinator of bicentennial programs at the Library of Congress from 1969 to 1971. Dr. Rutland is the author of many books including *Madison's Alternatives: The Jeffersonian Republicans and the Coming of War, 1805–1812, James Madison and the Search for Nationhood, James Madison: The Founding Father,* and *The Presidency of James Madison.* He is editor of *James Madison and the American Nation, 1751–1836: An Encyclopedia.*

Raymond W. Smock received his Ph.D. from the University of Maryland. He was involved with the Booker T. Washington Papers Project for many years and was coeditor from 1975 to 1983. He was Historian, Office of the Bicentennial, U.S. House of Representatives. In 1983, he was appointed as the first Director of the Office of the Historian of the U.S. House of Representatives. Among the major publications of that office are *The Biographical Directory of the United States Congress, 1774–1989, Black Americans in Congress, 1877–1989,* and *Women in Congress, 1917–1990.*

Darren D. Staloff received his Ph.D. from Columbia University, and he was a Post-Doctoral Fellow at the Institute of Early American History and Culture. He has taught at the College of Staten Island, Columbia University, and the College of William and Mary. Dr. Staloff is currently Assistant Professor of American History, The City College of the City University of New York. He is the author of *The Making of an American Thinking Class: Intellectuals and Intelligentsia in Puritan Massachusetts.*

John Stern received his M.A. from the State University of New York at Stony Brook, where he is enrolled in the doctoral program. His thesis is on Eugene McCarthy and the Presidential Campaign of 1968.

Edmund B. Sullivan received his Ed.D. from Fitchburg State College. He was Principal, New Hampton Community School, New Hampshire, and he taught at the North Adams and Newton public schools in Massachusetts. Dr. Sullivan was Professor at American International College and University of Hartford, and he was the founding Director and Curator of the Museum of American Political Life, West Hartford Connecticut. He is the author of *American Political Ribbons and Ribbon Badges, 1828–1988, American Political Badges and Medalets, 1789–1892,* and *Collecting Political Americana.*

Linda S. Vertrees received her B.A. in History from Western Illinois University and her M.A. in Library Science from the University of Chicago. She has written several annotated lists of suggested readings including the one for *The Holocaust, A Grolier Student Library.*

Thomas R. West received his Ph.D. from the Columbia University. He is Associate Professor, Department of History, Catholic University. He is coauthor, with David Burner, of *The Torch is Passed: The Kennedy Brothers and American Liberalism* and *Column Right: Conservative Journalists in the Service of Nationalism.*

INTRODUCTION

No branch of the federal government caused the authors of the Constitution as many problems as did the Executive. They feared a strong chief of state. After all, the American Revolution was, in part, a struggle against the King of England and the powerful royal governors. Surprisingly though, much power was granted to the president of the United States who is responsible only to the people. This was the boldest feature of the new Constitution. The president has varied duties. Above all, he must take care that the laws be faithfully executed. And also according to the Constitution, the president:

- is the commander in chief of the armed forces;
- has the power to make treaties with other nations (with the Senate's consent);
- appoints Supreme Court Justices and other members of the federal courts, ambassadors to other countries, department heads, and other high officials (all with the Senate's consent);
- signs into law or vetoes bills passed by Congress;
- calls special sessions of Congress in times of emergency.

In some countries, the power to lead is inherited. In others, men seize power through force. But in the United States, the people choose the nation's leader. The power of all the people to elect the president was not stated in the original Constitution. This came later. The United States is the first nation to have an elected president—and a president with a stated term of office. Every four years since the adoption of the Constitution in 1789, the nation has held a presidential election. Elections have been held even during major economic disruptions and wars. Indeed, these elections every four years are a vivid reminder of our democratic roots.

Who can vote for president of the United States? The original Constitution left voting qualifications to the states. At first, the states limited voting to white and very few black men who owned a certain amount of property. It was argued that only those with an economic or commercial interest in the nation should have a say in who could run the government. After the Civil War (1861–1865), the Fourteenth (1868) and Fifteenth (1870) Amendments to the Constitution guaranteed the vote to all men over the age of 21. The guarantee was only in theory. The Nineteenth Amendment (1920) extended the right to vote to women. The Nineteenth Amendment was a victory of the woman's suffrage movement which had worked for many years to achieve this goal. In 1964, the Twenty-fourth Amendment abolished poll taxes—a fee paid before a citizen was allowed to vote. This tax had kept many poor people, both black and white, from voting in several Southern states. And, the Twenty-sixth Amendment (1971) lowered the voting age to 18. (See Volume 8 for the complete text of the Constitution.)

In 1965, Congress passed the Voting Rights Act; it was renewed in 1985. This law, which carried out the requirements of the Fifteenth Amendment, made it illegal to interfere with anyone's right to vote. It forbade the use of literacy tests and, most important, the law mandated that federal voter registrars be sent into counties where less than 50 percent of the voting age population (black and white) was registered. This assumed that there must be serious barriers based on prejudice if so few had registered to vote. Those who had prevented African Americans from voting through fear and threat of violence now had to face the force of the federal government. Immediately, the number of African American voters in Southern states jumped dramatically from about 35 percent to 65 percent. In 1970, 1975, and 1982, Congress added amendments to the Voting Rights Act which helped other minorities such as Hispanics, Asians, Native Americans, and

Eskimos. For example, states must provide bilingual ballots in counties in which 5 percent or more of the population does not speak or read English. Today any citizen over the age of 18 has the right to vote in a presidential election. Many would argue that this is not only a right but also an obligation. However, all states deny the right to vote to anyone who is in prison.

Who can be president of the United States? There are formal constitutional requirements: one must be a "natural born citizen," at least 35 years old, and a resident of the United States for 14 years. The Constitution refers to the president as "he." It was probably beyond the thought process of the Founding Fathers that a woman, or a man who was not white, would ever be considered. The Twenty-second Amendment (1951), which deals with term limitations, uses "person" in referring to the president, recognizing that a woman could serve in that office.

How is the president elected? Most Americans assume that the president is elected by popular vote and the candidate with the highest number wins the election. This is not correct and may surprise those who thought they voted for Bill Clinton, Robert Dole, or Ross Perot in 1996. In fact, they voted for Clinton's or Dole's or Perot's electors who then elected the president. In the United States, the voters do not directly select the president. The Constitution provides a fairly complex—and some argue, an outdated—procedure for electing the president. Indeed, the electoral system devised by the Framers and modified by the Twelfth Amendment (1804) is unique. The records of the Constitutional Convention (1787) are silent in explaining the origins of the electoral system, usually referred to as the Electoral College. The several Federalist papers (Nos. 68–71) written by Alexander Hamilton in defense of the electoral system omit any source for the idea.

Under the electoral system of the United States, each state has the number of electoral voters equal to the size of its congressional delegation (House of Representatives plus Senate). Every 10 years, the census, as required by the Constitution, adjusts the number of representatives each state has in the House of Representatives because of population growth or loss. Every state always must have two senators. In the presidential election of 1996, for example, New York State had 33 electoral votes, because New York has 31 representatives and two senators. Alaska had three electoral votes, because Alaska has one representative and two senators. Since every congressional district must be approximately equal in population, we can say that the entire population of Alaska—the largest state in geographic size—is approximately equal in population to the 19th congressional district of New York City which covers the upper part of Manhattan Island.

There are 435 members of the House of Representatives. This number was fixed in 1910. There are 100 members of the Senate (50 states x 2 senators). This equals 535 electors. The Twenty-third Amendment (1961) gives the District of Columbia, the seat of our nation's capital, the electoral vote of the least populous state, three. So, the total electoral vote is 535 plus three or 538. To be elected president, a candidate must receive a majority, that is more than 50 percent, of the electoral votes: 270 electoral votes. If no candidate obtains a majority, the House of Representatives must choose the president from the top three candidates with each state delegation casting one vote. This happened in the 1824 presidential election. (See the article on John Quincy Adams.)

How does a political party choose its presidential nominee? Political parties play a crucial role—they select the candidates and provide the voters with a choice of alternatives.

In the early days of the Republic, the party's membership in Congress—the congressional caucus—chose presidential nominees. Sometimes state and local officials also put forward candidates. National party conventions where delegates were selected by state and local groups began by the 1830s. Each state had different delegate election procedures—some more democratic than others. Custom dictated that the convention sought the candidate. Potential nominees invariably seemed withdrawn and disinterested. They would rarely attend a nominating convention. Any attempt to pursue delegates was considered to be in bad taste. In fact, custom dictated that an official delegation went to the nominee's home to notify him of the party's decision and ask if he would accept. In the early years, convention officials sent a letter. By 1852, the candidate was informed in person. In the 1890s, these notification ceremonies dramatically increased in size. Madison Square Garden in New York City was the site for Grover Cleveland's 1892 notification.

By the first decade of the twentieth century, political reformers considered the convention system most undemocratic. They felt that it was a system dominated by patronage seeking party bosses who ignored the average voter. The primary system began as a way to increase participation in the nominating process. Candidates for the nation's highest office now actually sought the support of convention delegates. Theoretically, the primary allows all party members to choose their party's nominee. Most twentieth century conventions though, have seen a combination of delegates chosen by a political machine and elected in a primary. Today success in the primaries virtually assures the nomination. With few exceptions, the national conventions have become a rubber stamp for the candidate who did the best in the primaries.

The Campaign and Election. The presidential campaign is the great democratic exercise in politics. In recent elections, televised debates between the candidates have become a ritual, attracting record numbers of viewers. Public opinion polls continually monitor the nation's pulse. Commentators and writers analyze campaign strategies. Perhaps the winning strategy is to mobilize the party faithful and to persuade the independent voter that their candidate is the best. This is a costly process and since 1976, the general treasury provides major financial assistance to presidential campaigns. Public funding helps serious presidential candidates to present their qualifications without selling out to wealthy contributors and special interest groups.

Finally, on that first Tuesday after the first Monday in November, the voters make their choice. With the tragic exception of 1860, the American people have accepted the results. (See the article on Abraham Lincoln.) The election process works. Democracy has survived. Forty-one men have held the office of president of the United States. Each has been a powerful personality with varied leadership traits. Each had the opportunity to make major decisions both in foreign and domestic matters which affected the direction of the nation.

Join us as we proceed to study the men who helped to shape our history. We will also learn about their vice presidents, their cabinets, their families, and their homes and monuments.

Fred L. Israel
The City College of the City University of New York

ACKNOWLEDGMENTS

Sir Isaac Newton, the seventeenth-century English scientist who created calculus, discovered that white light is composed of many colors, discovered the law of gravity, and developed the standard laws of motion, once said, "If I have seen farther, it is because I have stood on the shoulders of giants." He meant that he used the work of those who came before him as a starting point for the development of his own ideas. This concept is as true in reference books as it is in science.

The White House Historical Association (740 Jackson Place N.W., Washington, D.C. 20503) supplied all the full page color paintings of the presidents, except seven. They are used with the permission of the White House

Historical Association, and we are grateful to them for their cooperation. The painting of James Monroe is Courtesy of the James Monroe Museum and Memorial Library, Fredericksburg, Virginia; the William Henry Harrison portrait is Courtesy of Grouseland; the John Tyler painting is Courtesy of Sherwood Forest Plantation; the Benjamin Harrison painting is from the President Benjamin Harrison Home; Harry Truman's photograph is from the U.S. Navy, Courtesy Harry S. Truman Library; George Bush's photograph is Courtesy of the Bush Presidential Materials Project; Bill Clinton's photograph is Courtesy of The White House. All the busts of the vice presidents are Courtesy of the Architect of the Capitol.

Over three dozen illustrations are credited to the Collection of David J. and Janice L. Frent. The Frents are friends and neighbors. Fred Israel and I both want to thank them very much for allowing us to show some of the treasures of their unequaled collection of political memorabilia.

The authors of the biographical pieces on the presidents are listed in each volume. They have provided the core of this work, and I am very grateful to them for their cooperation. Dr. Donald A. Ritchie, Associate Historian, United States Senate, wrote all the biographies of the vice presidents. Few people know more about this subject than Dr. Ritchie, and we appreciate his assistance.

Maribeth A. Corona (Editor, Charles E. Smith Books, Inc.) and I have written the sections on Family, Cabinet, and Places. Dr. Israel's editing of our work corrected and improved it greatly although we take full responsibility for any errors that remain. In preparing the material on places, three books served as a starting point: *Presidential Libraries and Museums, An Illustrated Guide,* Pat Hyland (Congressional Quarterly Inc., 1995); *Historic Homes of the American Presidents,* second edition, Irvin Haas (Dover Publications, 1991); and *Cabins, Cottages & Mansions, Homes of the Presidents of the United States,* Nancy D. Myers Benbow and Christopher H. Benbow (Thomas Publications, 1993). We wrote to every place noted in this work and our copy is based on the wealth of information returned to us. It is the most comprehensive and up-to-date collection of information available on this subject.

There is no single book on the families of the presidents. We relied on the abundance of biographies and autobiographies of members of the first families. Also helpful was *Children in the White House,* Christine Sadler (G.P. Putnam's Sons, 1967); *The Presidents' Mothers,* Doris Faber (St. Martin's Press, 1978); and *The First Ladies,* Margaret Brown Klapthor (White House Historical Association, 1989).

The Complete Book of U.S. Presidents, William A. DeGregorio (Wings Books, 1993) is an outstanding one-volume reference work, and we referred to it often. I also had the great pleasure of referring often to three encyclopedias which I had published earlier: *Encyclopedia of the American Presidency,* Leonard W. Levy and Louis Fisher (Simon & Schuster, 1994); *Encyclopedia of the American Constitution,* Leonard W. Levy, Kenneth L. Karst, and Dennis Mahoney (Macmillan & Free Press, 1986); and *Encyclopedia of the United States Congress,* Donald C. Bacon, Roger Davidson, and Morton H. Keller (Simon & Schuster, 1995). I also referred often to *Running for President, The Candidates and Their Images,* Arthur M. Schlesinger, Jr. (Simon & Schuster, 1994). Publishing this two-volume set also gave me the pleasure of working with Professor Schlesinger and the Associate Editors, Fred L. Israel and David J. Frent.

Most of the copyediting was done by Jerilyn Famighetti who was, as usual, prompt, accurate, and pleasant. Our partner in this endeavor was M.E. Aslett Corporation, 95 Campus Plaza, Edison, New Jersey. Although everyone at Aslett lent a hand, special thanks go to Elizabeth Geary, who designed the books; Brian Hewitt and Bob Bovasso, who scanned the images; and Joanne Morbit, who composed the pages. They designed every page and prepared the film for printing. The index was prepared by Jacqueline Flamm.

Charles E. Smith
Freehold, New Jersey

Zachary Taylor

12TH PRESIDENT

OF THE UNITED STATES OF AMERICA

CHRONOLOGICAL EVENTS

24 November 1784	Born, Orange County, Virginia
3 May 1808	Commissioned first lieutenant, Seventh Infantry Regiment, U.S. Army
November 1810	Promoted to captain
18 June 1812	War with Great Britain declared (War of 1812)
31 October 1812	Promoted to brevet major
24 December 1814	Treaty of Ghent signed, ending war with Great Britain
20 April 1819	Promoted to lieutenant colonel
5 April 1832	Promoted to colonel
May–August 1832	Fought in Black Hawk War
January 1838	Promoted to brevet brigadier general for heroism against Seminoles in the Battle of Okeechobee
15 May 1838	Appointed commanding officer of all U.S. forces in Florida
June 1845	Commanded Army of Occupation on Mexican border
8–9 May 1846	Victory at Battles of Palo Alto and Resaca de la Palma
13 May 1846	War with Mexico declared
29 June 1846	Promoted to major general
23–24 February 1847	Victory at Battle of Buena Vista
2 February 1848	Treaty of Guadalupe Hildalgo signed, ending war with Mexico
7 November 1848	Elected president
5 March 1849	Inaugurated president
19 April 1850	Clayton-Bulwer Treaty signed
9 July 1850	Died, Washington, D.C.

BIOGRAPHY

Zachary Taylor stuttered and he was a terrible speller. He seemed incapable of writing a coherent paragraph. He preferred old clothes to smart military uniforms. He waddled rather than walked and wore floppy old straw hats. He was hardly the figure of a man who would become this country's twelfth president.

OLD ROUGH AND READY. Zachary Taylor was a successful general of unquestioned courage and honesty. He had a reputation for fairness in military administration and originality in leadership. His string of widely acclaimed victories during the war with Mexico (1846–1848) made him a national hero. Even before the war was over, both Democrats and Whigs approached him to be a candidate for the White House in 1848. He was "Old Rough and Ready" to his troops and an admiring public.

He had no previous political experience, and he had never voted. However, his admirers were not discouraged. He was strictly a military man, he fre-

Zachary Taylor served in the army for 40 years, from 1808 to 1848. He served in the War of 1812, the Black Hawk War (1832), the Second Seminole War (1837–1840), and the Mexican War (1846–1848). He became a national hero after his defeat of General Antonio Lopez de Santa Ana at the Battle of Buena Vista. (Courtesy National Archives.)

quently explained, and he was much too busy to vote. Soldiering, not politics, he would add, was his life. He was never in one place long enough to vote. His victories over the Mexican armies at Palo Alto, Resaca de la Palma, Buena Vista, and Monterey convinced many voters that lack of involvement in politics was not a handicap. Battlefield heroics were an influential starting point on the road to the White House, as with George Washington, Andrew Jackson, and William Henry Harrison. Only two other presidents, Ulysses S. Grant and Dwight D. Eisenhower, won the presidency without any previous political experience.

Zachary Taylor was born on 24 November 1784 in Orange County, Virginia. He lived in Louisiana for most of his life and considered it his home state. He was a southerner who owned slaves and two plantations. As a presidential candidate, however, he firmly opposed extending slavery into the territories. He defended this seeming contradiction by arguing that the Constitution should prohibit slavery beyond those states where it was already legal. That is, he advocated an anti-slavery amendment to the Constitution. He refused to support proposals which mandated popular or "squatter" sovereignty for the new territories taken from Mexico.

How did Zachary Taylor win the White House? Certainly his wartime exploits gave him an advantage, but they alone did not guarantee victory.

In May 1846, Zachary Taylor defeated a Mexican force at Resaca de la Palma. For this victory, he was promoted to major general. (Courtesy National Archives.)

> "Your remarks in relation to my being a candidate for the Presidency are very flattering, but I think you well know without the necessity of saying so to you that I am not and shall never be an aspirant for that honor. My opinion has always been against the elevation of a military chief to that position."
>
> • *Zachary Taylor told General Thomas Young his thoughts on running for the presidency in a letter of 18 July 1846. At that time, Taylor was serving in the Mexican War.*

Major party leaders tried to contain and play down slavery and sectionalism, but the controversy was becoming hard to ignore by 1848. The abolitionist movement, scorned in its earlier years, was gaining more public support. The Democratic Party was breaking apart, as conservative Southerners fought with liberal Northerners. This pattern continues to plague it to this day. The Democratic candidate was Governor Lewis Cass of Michigan. He was a veteran of the War of 1812, as was Taylor, and a highly regarded administrator. He was a defender of the right of new settlers, or squatters, to decide for themselves whether to vote their new territory slave or free.

Henry Clay, then over 70 years of age, made his fourth bid for the Whig nomination. Many Whigs regarded him more as a memory of the past than as a real flesh and blood candidate. The other candidates were Winfield Scott and Daniel Webster. Taylor had the reluctant support of such prominent Whigs as journalist Horace Greeley and the influential Massachusetts Senator Daniel Webster. Webster had argued earlier that Taylor was not fit for the nomination, but he later supported him. He said that "[he] is an honest man whom I would trust on the matter of slavery."

Despite his opposition to the Mexican War, Congressman Abraham Lincoln was an enthusiastic supporter of Taylor. Lincoln spoke frequently during the campaign, most notably in his famous "military coattails" speech in the U.S. House of Representatives in July 1848. Lincoln made fun of Cass and referred humorously to his own brief service during the Black Hawk War. Lincoln later turned down President Taylor's offer to appoint him governor of Oregon Territory as a reward for his services in the campaign.

FREE STATE OR SLAVE. The emergence of the Free Soil Party was equally important in explaining Taylor's victory. The Free Soil Party was made up mostly of Northern Democrats who strongly opposed extending slavery into the territories. They disagreed with their party's nominee, former President Martin Van Buren, for his acceptance of the squatter sovereignty position. Van Buren, still a prominent Democrat, was well known for his opposition to slavery. The Free Soil Party also attracted members of the Liberty Party whose sole aim was the abolition of slavery. They judged correctly that Van Buren would get more votes than their own candidate, John Hale of New Hampshire.

Third parties tend to have a spoiler role in U.S. politics. They do not win but they spoil things for the other parties. The 1848 campaign was no exception. In the fall election, New York gave more votes to Van Buren than to Cass. The combined votes of Van Buren and Cass topped Taylor's number of votes by over 15,000. It is not certain that Cass would have won New York with its 36 electoral votes had the Free Soilers not been a factor, but it is very likely. Similarly, Pennsylvania, considered safe for Cass, gave Taylor its 26 electoral votes.

In the final analysis, it was likely that Taylor himself was the direct cause of his victory. His frequent responses to all who wrote him were usually long explanations of why he was a plain living, simple man who was more at home on the battlefield than in political office. Local newspapers followed the custom of printing these responses. Other than his earlier stated opposition to extend-

The Whigs held their Convention in Philadelphia in June 1848. Zachary Taylor won the nomination. Daniel Webster (pictured here) came in fourth behind Taylor, Henry Clay, and Winfield Scott. (Courtesy Library of Congress.)

Zachary Taylor and Millard Fillmore, the Whig candidates, received 163 electoral votes to 127 electoral votes for the Democratic candidates Lewis Cass and William O. Butler. (Courtesy Collection of David J. and Janice L. Frent.)

Lewis Cass and William O. Butler, the Democratic candidates, received 42.5 percent of the popular vote. Zachary Taylor and Millard Fillmore received 47.4 percent of the popular vote. The Free Soil candidates, Martin Van Buren and Charles Francis Adams received 10.1 percent of the popular vote. (Courtesy Collection of David J. and Janice L. Frent.)

INAUGURAL ADDRESS

. . . The confidence and respect shown by my countrymen in calling me to be the chief magistrate of a Republic holding a high rank among the nations of the earth have inspired me with feelings of the most profound gratitude; but when I reflect that the acceptance of the office which their partiality has bestowed imposes the discharge of the most arduous duties and involves the weightiest obligations, I am conscious that the position which I have been called to fill, though sufficient to satisfy the loftiest ambition, is surrounded by fearful responsibilities. Happily, however, in the performance of my new duties I shall not be without able cooperation. The legislative and judicial branches of the government present prominent examples of distinguished civil attainments and matured experience, and it shall be my endeavor to call to my assistance in the executive departments individuals whose talents, integrity, and purity of character will furnish ample guarantees for the faithful and honorable performance of the trusts to be committed to their charge. With such aids and an honest purpose to do whatever is right, I hope to execute diligently, impartially, and for the best interests of the country the manifold duties devolved upon me. . . .

As American freemen we cannot but sympathize in all efforts to extend the blessings of civil and political liberty, but at the same time we are warned by the admonitions of history and the voice of our own beloved Washington to abstain from entangling alliances with foreign nations. In all disputes between conflicting governments it is our interest not less than our duty to remain strictly neutral, while our geographical position, the genius of our institutions and our people, the advancing spirit of civilization, and, above all, the dictates of religion direct us to the cultivation of peaceful and friendly relations with all other powers. . . . In the conduct of our foreign relations I shall conform to these views, as I believe them essential to the best interests and the true honor of the country. . . .

It shall be my study to recommend such constitutional measures to Congress as may be necessary and proper to secure encouragement and protection to the great interests of agriculture, commerce, and manufacturers, to improve our rivers and harbors, to provide for the speedy extinguishment of the public debt, to enforce a strict accountability on the part of all officers of the government and the utmost economy in all public expenditures; but it is for the wisdom of Congress itself, in which all legislative powers are vested by the Constitution, to regulate these and other matters of domestic policy. I shall look with confidence to the enlightened patriotism of that body to adopt such measures of conciliation as may harmonize conflicting interests and tend to perpetuate that Union which should be the paramount object of our hopes and affections. In any action calculated to promote an object so near the heart of everyone who truly loves his country I will zealously unite with the coordinate branches of the government. . . .

• *For the second time since the adoption of the Constitution, the end of a presidential term fell on a Sunday. Zachary Taylor's inauguration, therefore, took place in front of the Capitol on Monday, 5 March 1849. Retiring President James K. Polk talked with Taylor about national problems during their ride to the ceremonies. In the evening, Polk wrote in his diary that the General impressed him as a well-meaning old man, but "exceedingly ignorant of public affairs, and, I should judge, of very ordinary capacity."*

FIRST ANNUAL MESSAGE

. . . No civil government having been provided by Congress for California, the people of that territory, impelled by the necessities of their political condition, recently met in convention for the purpose of forming a constitution and state government, which the latest advices give me reason to suppose has been accomplished; and it is believed they will shortly apply for the admission of California into the Union as a sovereign state. Should such be the case, and should their constitution be conformable to the requisitions of the Constitution of the United States, I recommend their application to the favorable consideration of Congress. The people of New Mexico will also, it is believed, at no very distant period present themselves for admission into the Union. Preparatory to the admission of California and New Mexico the people of each will have instituted for themselves a republican form of government, "laying its foundation in such principles and organizing its powers in such form as to them shall seem most likely to effect their safety and happiness." By awaiting their action all causes of uneasiness may be avoided and confidence and kind feeling preserved. With a view of maintaining the harmony and tranquillity so dear to all, we should abstain from the introduction of those exciting topics of a sectional character which have hitherto produced painful apprehensions in the public mind; and I repeat the solemn warning of the first and most illustrious of my predecessors against furnishing "any ground for characterizing parties by geographical discriminations." . . .

• *President Taylor delivered his first Annual Message to Congress on 24 December 1849. It is said that it was drafted by Secretary of State John M. Clayton. Congress's major problem during Taylor's administration was the preservation of the Union. The number of slave and free states were the same at that time. Taylor, himself a slaveholder, recommended that California be admitted as a free state.*

ing slavery, he made no commitments and raised no controversies. He rejected any deals.

Taylor displayed a native political shrewdness and insight into the electoral process which was entirely at odds with his military background. He appeared disinterested in politics before his nomination and in the campaign itself. This created the image of ordinary citizen seeking the nation's highest office in the name of the people. The fact that he was a popular war hero was enough for many voters. The American people gave him the presidency by a narrow margin of 139,000 votes.

THE PRESIDENCY. Many voters had a vague idea of what President Taylor was against but few knew what he was for. Many probably agreed with New England author James Russell Lowell's judgment in 1848 in *The Bigelow Papers* (in rural dialect):

> Another pint that informs the minds of
>   sober jedges

> Is that the Gin'ral hazn't gut tied hand
>   an' foot with pledges;
> He hazn't told ye wut he is, so there ain't
>   no knowin';
> But wut he may turn out to be, the best
>   there is agoin'

Taylor did have strong opinions concerning sectionalism and slavery, the major controversies of his administration. Sectionalism and slavery refer to the tendency of states to emphasize in Congress their distinctive economic and social interests over other sections of the country and to vote accordingly. He encouraged the recently added California territories to apply for statehood. He expected them to enter the Union as free states. This would help to prevent the further expansion of slavery. Growing numbers of fortune seekers were attracted to California by the discovery of gold early in 1848. The U.S. military government and

CLAYTON-BULWER TREATY

I herewith transmit to the Senate, for their advice with regard to its ratification, a convention between the United States and Great Britain, concluded at Washington on the 19th instant by John M. Clayton, Secretary of State, on the part of the United States, and by the Right Hon. Sir Henry Lytton Bulwer, on the part of Great Britain.

This treaty has been negotiated in accordance with the general views expressed in my message to Congress in December last. Its object is to establish a commercial alliance with all great maritime states for the protection of a contemplated ship canal through the territory of Nicaragua to connect the Atlantic and Pacific oceans, and at the same time to insure the same protection to the contemplated railways or canals by the Tehuantepec and Panama routes, as well as to every other interoceanic communication which may be adopted to shorten the transit to or from our territories on the Pacific.

It will be seen that this treaty does not propose to take money from the public Treasury to effect any object contemplated by it. It yields protection to the capitalists who may undertake to construct any canal or railway across the Isthmus, commencing in the southern part of Mexico and terminating in the territory of New Granada. It gives no preference to any one route over another, but proposes the same measure of protection for all which ingenuity and enterprise can construct. Should this treaty be ratified, it will secure in future the liberation of all Central America from any kind of foreign aggression.

At the time negotiations were opened with Nicaragua for the construction of a canal through her territory I found Great Britain in possession of nearly half of Central America, as the ally and protector of the Mosquito King. It has been my object in negotiating this treaty not only to secure the passage across the Isthmus to the Government and citizens of the United States by the construction of a great highway dedicated to the use of all nations on equal terms, but to maintain the independence and sovereignty of all the Central American Republics. The Senate will judge how far these objects have been effected. . . .

• *An important step toward the building of the Panama Canal was taken under President Taylor's administration. The 1850 Clayton-Bulwer Treaty calmed fierce competition between the United States and Great Britain as both nations agreed never to obtain exclusive control over a ship canal.*

John M. Clayton and Henry Lytton Bulwer signed the treaty on 19 April 1850. President Taylor submitted it to the U.S. Senate within a few days. The Senate passed it by a vote of 42 to 11. President Taylor proclaimed the treaty from his deathbed on 5 July 1850. The treaty was widely criticized because it gave too much to Great Britain, but the only alternative would have been war. The Hay-Pauncefote Treaties of 1900 and 1901 nullified this treaty and gave the United States the sole right to build and control a canal.

what was left of the Mexican administration were not able to maintain any degree of law and order. Intense lobbying in Congress was another factor that led to the admission of California in 1850, after Taylor's death.

President Taylor was a traditional Whig. He viewed the executive branch as deferring to the legislative in most matters. As president, he made it clear that he was a nationalist before he was a southerner or a sectionalist. He believed that the well-being of the country was most important, not that of one section over another. As a general, he might have reasoned, he led an American army; as president, he would lead an American nation.

A NATION MOURNS
A NATION'S LOSS

Z. Taylor

PEOPLES THE CHOICE

INAUGURATED MARCH 5TH
1849.

DIED JULY 9TH 1850.

AGED 66 YEARS

When Texas wanted to expand its boundaries by adding New Mexico Territory, Taylor threatened to send in federal troops to prevent this from happening. He likewise threatened to blockade southern ports if those states seceded. This is precisely what President Abraham Lincoln would do a decade later. Taylor's actions increasingly alienated him from his southern supporters and tested his overall support. He was, after all, a general. He was accustomed to making binding decisions which, if necessary, he would carry out himself.

Zachary Taylor was not a compromiser. Like most presidents who served between Andrew Jackson and Abraham Lincoln, he was powerless to prevent the progress of the twin evils of slavery and sectionalism. Compromises, such as those offered by Henry Clay, were only temporary substitutes to prevent armed confrontation. Taylor was obstinate and strong-willed. Compromise of any sort was impossible for him.

Perhaps some political experience would have made a difference, especially the ability to appreciate that compromise was sometimes needed. However, he held firm regarding the fundamental, indeed central, controversies of his presidency: slavery and sectionalism. Perhaps he was moving toward some peaceful resolution. Perhaps he was learning to be president. We can never know. Old Rough and Ready died in office on 9 July 1850 after having served just 16 months. He died apparently of acute gastroenteritis, which is inflammation of the stomach and intestines. This disease was a killer in Taylor's day because of the lack of understanding of how viruses and bacteria contaminate food and water supplies.

The design of this ribbon was used for the 1849 inauguration of Zachary Taylor. The top and bottom inscriptions were added after his death and the ribbon was reissued as a memorial piece.
(Courtesy Collection of David J. and Janice L. Frent.)

VICE PRESIDENT

Fillmore moved to Buffalo in 1830 to open a law practice. An outgoing man, he polished his manners and dressed stylishly. He came to the attention of the state political leader, Thurlow Weed, who helped him win election to the New York State Assembly and to the U.S. House of Representatives. In Congress, Fillmore endorsed Henry Clay's "American System" of internal improvements, tariffs, and a national bank. When the new Whig Party gained the majority in 1841, Fillmore ran for Speaker of the House. Placing second, he instead chaired the powerful Committee on Ways and Means. As chairman, he sponsored the Tariff of 1842, a key part of the Whig Party's legislative agenda.

Considered for vice president in 1844, Fillmore had a falling out with Thurlow Weed, who backed another candidate. The Whigs were defeated in 1844, but their fortunes reversed during the Mexican War. In 1848, the Whigs nominated General Zachary Taylor of Louisiana, a war hero, for president. For balance, they chose Fillmore for vice president. Fillmore helped the ticket carry New York and with it the election.

Debating the future of the territories acquired by the war, Northerners and Southerners violently disagreed on whether to permit slavery in the West. Senator Henry Clay introduced a compromise with provisions to appease both supporters and opponents of slavery. Vice President Fillmore presided over the emotionally charged debates over Clay's compromise.

President Taylor, who was hostile to the compromise, died on 9 July 1850. Becoming president, Fillmore threw his support behind settling the territorial issue and signed the compromise into law. The Compromise of 1850 proved only a temporary settlement, however, which weakened the Whig Party. Fillmore wanted to run in 1852, but the Whigs turned instead to General Winfield Scott. Scott lost, and the Whigs never again elected a president. In 1856, Fillmore campaigned for president on the Know-Nothing ticket but finished a distant third in the election. He retired from politics to serve as chancellor of the University of Buffalo.

Millard Fillmore
(1800–1874)

CHRONOLOGICAL EVENTS

1800	Born, Locke Township, New York, 7 January
1828	Elected to New York State Assembly
1832	Elected to U.S. House of Representatives
1847	Elected comptroller of New York
1848	Elected vice president
1850	Became president upon the death of Zachary Taylor
1856	Ran unsuccessfully for president
1874	Died, Buffalo, New York, March 8

BIOGRAPHY

One of 9 children of a poor farm family, Millard Fillmore spent his childhood on the farm and received little schooling. Apprenticed to a textile mill, he taught himself to read. Then he attended school in New Hope, New York, where he met and married the local minister's daughter, Abigail Powers. By teaching school, he earned enough to buy out the remaining time of his apprenticeship.

THE CABINET

SECRETARY OF STATE
John M. Clayton, 1849

SECRETARY OF WAR
George W. Crawford, 1849

SECRETARY OF THE TREASURY
William M. Meredith, 1849

POSTMASTER GENERAL
Jacob Collamer, 1849

ATTORNEY GENERAL
Isaac Toucey, 1849
Reverdy Johnson, 1849

SECRETARY OF THE NAVY
William B. Preston, 1849

SECRETARY OF THE INTERIOR[1]
Thomas Ewing, 1849

1. Department of the Interior established 3 March 1849.

(Courtesy U.S. Naval Historical Center.)

William B. Preston (1805–1862). Preston was appointed secretary of the navy by President Zachary Taylor in 1849. He had previously served as a representative from Virginia in the U.S. House of Representatives (1846–1849).

Although Preston came from the South, he opposed slavery and favored its gradual abolition. He also supported the admission of California as a free state. Preston served briefly as secretary of the navy until the cabinet was reorganized by President Millard Fillmore in July 1850. He resumed his law practice and gained a state-wide reputation as a defense lawyer.

Preston initially opposed the secession of Virginia. Probably for that reason he was chosen to present the ordinance of secession for Virginia to emphasize the necessity of the action. After the secession of Southern states from the Union, Preston was elected to the Confederate States Congress in which he served until his death in 1862.

FAMILY

CHRONOLOGICAL EVENTS

21 September 1788	Margaret (Peggy) Mackall Smith born	20 April 1824	Daughter, Mary Elizabeth (Betty), born
21 June 1810	Peggy Smith married Zachary Taylor	27 January 1826	Son, Richard (Dick), born
		1835	Daughter, Sarah Knox, died
9 April 1811	Daughter, Ann, born	9 July 1850	Zachary Taylor died
6 March 1814	Daughter, Sarah Knox, born	August 1852	Peggy Taylor died

(Courtesy Library of Congress.)

The Taylors had three daughters and a son live to maturity. Two daughters died in infancy.

Ann married Dr. Robert C. Wood, an army surgeon. They were stationed in Baltimore so Taylor's four grandchildren were frequent visitors to the White House.

At the age of 21, Sarah Knox Taylor married Jefferson Davis, the future president of the Confederacy, even though her father objected strongly. She died several months later from malaria.

The youngest daughter, Betty (pictured here), married Colonel William Bliss. He was her father's confidential secretary. She served as President Taylor's official hostess because the First Lady was very ill.

Dick Taylor was a general in the Confederate army during the Civil War.

ZACHARY TAYLOR NATIONAL CEMETERY

4701 Brownsboro Road • Louisville, Kentucky 40207 • Tel: (502) 893-3852

> *Open daily. No admission fee. Administered by the National Cemetery System, Department of Veterans Affairs.*

The mausoleum is limestone, with the interior lined in marble. The inscription "1784 Zachary Taylor 1850" appears over the two glass-paneled bronze doors. The original family vault can still be seen in the family burial grounds. (Courtesy National Cemetery System, Department of Veterans Affairs.) ▶

A granite shaft that supports a marble statue of President Taylor is located approximately 30 feet from the mausoleum. This memorial shaft was erected by the State of Kentucky in 1883. Its base is inscribed with President Taylor's dying words: "I have endeavored to do my duty, I am ready to die." (Courtesy National Cemetery System, Department of Veterans Affairs.) ▶

In the spring of 1785, Zachary Taylor's father, Colonel Richard Taylor, received a bonus of land from the government for his service in the Revolutionary War. The 400-acre Taylor family farm in Jefferson County, Kentucky, came to be known as Springfield. Zachary Taylor grew to adulthood there. In 1801, he left to pursue a career in the United States Army. The home is privately owned and not open to the public.

After President Taylor's death in 1850, his remains were placed in a vault located on the Taylor Farm Burial Grounds at Springfield. They were transferred from the vault to a mausoleum, erected on the property by the United States Government, in May 1926.

The cemetery is the only site commemorating President Taylor that is open to the public. It was officially named the Zachary Taylor National Cemetery by an Act of Congress approved on 10 May 1928 and by General Orders, War Department, in 1936. The Taylor Family Burial Grounds, consisting of approximately half an acre, is located within the confines of the national cemetery. Although the burial grounds are privately owned, the area is cared for and maintained by the United States Government out of respect for the former president.

Millard Fillmore

13TH PRESIDENT
OF THE UNITED STATES OF AMERICA

CHRONOLOGICAL EVENTS

7 January 1800	Born, Locke Township, Cayuga County, New York
1819	Became law clerk
1823	Admitted to bar, Erie County, New York
13 November 1828	Elected to New York State Assembly
1832	Elected to U.S. House of Representatives
1835	Retired from politics; practiced law
1836	Again elected to U.S. House of Representatives
1838 and 1840	Reelected to U.S. House of Representatives
1841	Appointed chairman of House Ways and Means Committee
1842	Drafted Tariff Act of 1842
1844	Ran unsuccessfully for governor of New York
1847	Elected comptroller of New York
7 November 1848	Elected vice president
9 July 1850	Became president upon the death of Zachary Taylor
9 September 1850	Signed act establishing Territories of New Mexico and Utah
17 September 1850	Compromise of 1850 became law
18 September 1850	Signed Fugitive Slave Act
1852	Dispatched expedition to Japan under the command of Commodore Matthew C. Perry
April 1852	Retired to Buffalo, New York
4 November 1856	Defeated for election as president
8 March 1874	Died, Buffalo, New York

BIOGRAPHY

EARLY LIFE. Millard Fillmore, the thirteenth president of the United States, was born in Cayuga County, New York, on 7 January 1800. In the early decades of the nineteenth century, western New York was the frontier, and the Fillmores were among the thousands of New Englanders who had begun to migrate there. Millard, the first of five sons of Nathaniel and Phoebe Fillmore, spent his early years doing chores on the family farm.

Fillmore received no formal schooling until he was 18, but he learned the basics of reading, writing, and arithmetic from the family Bible and almanac. At age 14, he became an apprentice at a cloth mill. When he was 17, he joined a local circulating library and began to read everything he could lay his hands on. Fillmore enrolled at an academy that opened nearby. There he met and fell in love with his future wife, Abigail Powers, the daughter of a Methodist minister.

Fillmore had no love of clothmaking, so he was

overjoyed when his father arranged for him to become a legal clerk. Moving west to Buffalo, he continued his legal studies while teaching grade school. Recognizing his legal talents, several older members of the bar in 1823 persuaded the Court of Common Pleas to admit Fillmore to practice, despite his studying for only two years rather than the customary seven.

NEW YORK STATE ASSEMBLY. For the next five years, Fillmore built a thriving legal practice. In 1828, he entered politics, winning a seat in the state assembly on the Anti-Masonic ticket. The antimasonic movement had begun in Batavia, New York, in 1826, when William Morgan, a local stonemason, disappeared after threatening to publish a book revealing the secrets of Freemasonry.

The Masonic Order was a secret society dating back to the Middle Ages. Many prominent Americans were Masons, including a number of the Founding Fathers. The Order was portrayed by its enemies as a sinister conspiracy. They claimed that Masonry had no respect for the laws of the nation, and that members of the Order were manipulating society for their own evil purposes. They alleged that Masons had murdered Morgan to silence him.

Guided by the influential newspaper publisher Thurlow Weed, antimasonry became a political party. In the late 1820s U.S. politics centered on two rivals—John Quincy Adams and Andrew Jackson. The Anti-Masonic Party had in fact been created by Weed as a tool of the Adams supporters.

Fillmore served three terms in the New York State Assembly, where he successfully sponsored a bill ending imprisonment for debt. Fillmore was able to persuade assemblymen on all sides, but especially Democrats, that reform of debt law to prevent the jailing of debtors and to create mechanisms for the declaration of bankruptcy would benefit all. This early experience at negotiating a successful compromise between opponents influenced his entire future political career.

UNITED STATES CONGRESS. In 1832, Fillmore was elected to the U.S. House of Representatives as an Anti-Jacksonian. By this time antimasonism had largely burned out, since it was a one-issue movement based on opposition to a conspiracy that could not be proved. For men like Fillmore the more important issues dealt with principles that placed them squarely against President Jackson. They believed that the government should aid groups who could make the nation prosper. It should do this by providing sound currency and protection for business and by encouraging investment in projects such as canals and railroads. These men forged the coalition of Anti-Masons and New Republicans that became the Whig Party.

In 1834, Fillmore left office to help build the new party. He returned to the U.S. House of Representatives in 1836 although the Whig candidate for president, William Henry Harrison, lost to Democrat Martin Van Buren. Van Buren's financial policies soon backfired, plunging the nation into depression. Whigs won important electoral victories in 1838, with great prospects for success in the coming presidential elections.

In the 1838 elections, a new issue began to take prominence, as antislavery forces, called abolitionists, lobbied Whig candidates for support. In response to their inquiries, Fillmore stated plainly that he was against slavery, but refused to make any promises of action. But as this issue intensified throughout the next two decades it would become impossible to ignore.

The Whigs won an overwhelming victory in 1840, placing William Henry Harrison in the White House. Harrison died very soon after the election and was succeeded by his vice president, Virginian John Tyler. Fillmore, by then an important figure in the Whig Party, was deeply involved in the infighting between the congressional Whig majority and the increasingly stubborn and independent President. He became chairman of the Ways and Means Committee, responsible for directing the finances of the nation.

Fillmore was extremely active in this role, drafting and promoting into law the Tariff Act of 1842, protectionist legislation benefiting U.S. manufacturing interests. Tariffs were favored by abolitionists as well, who believed that trade restrictions put pressure on Southern slaveholders, who were very dependent upon overseas trade and products. Whigs were happy to accept credit for the easing of the depression, whether or not the tariff was really responsible for the upturn. Despite the acclaim Fillmore received, he decided to retire from Congress.

RETURN TO NEW YORK. Always torn between national interests and the local concerns of New York, Fillmore had grown increasingly anxious about two movements that threatened the Whig coalition at home. In western New York, Fillmore's own region, the abolitionist Liberty Party was growing in strength. In and around the city of New York, anti-Catholic "nativism" was making deep inroads into the Whig Party.

The emerging nativism took several forms. Some argued that immigrants created urban slums and corrupted politics by selling their votes. Others complained that immigrants were willing to work for low wages and were taking jobs from the native born. Protestants feared the Irish Catholics' success in politics, and Whig politicians were enraged that immigrants tended to vote Democratic. As Whig fortunes faltered in Washington, Fillmore decided that he could accomplish more by trying to reinvigorate the Whig Party in New York.

His retirement did not last long. In 1843, Fillmore sought the Whig nomination for vice president. His plans were at cross purposes to those of New York State Whig leaders, especially Thurlow Weed, who had decided that Fillmore could best serve the party by running for governor. When he failed to win the Whig vice presidential nomination in 1844, Fillmore had no choice but to accept the nomination for governor of New York.

Fillmore's Democratic opponent, Silas Wright, effectively used fear of nativist influence in the Whig Party to recruit many immigrant voters to his side, especially Catholics. Meanwhile, abolitionists objected to the Whig candidate for president, Henry Clay, a Kentucky slaveholder. The great issue of the election was the proposed annexation of Texas. Abolitionists were strongly opposed to the entry of that vast slaveholding region into the United States. While Fillmore and other Whigs were strongly against the annexation of Texas, the party as a whole was less willing to make a forceful stand on the issue, and this drove abolitionists from their ranks. The Whigs lost badly in 1844. Fillmore lost his bid to become governor of New York. Convinced that this defeat was the result of the opposition of immigrants and abolitionists, his sentiments began to turn more nativist.

After three years of private life, Fillmore was elected New York State Comptroller in 1847. As the state's chief financial administrator, Fillmore once again came to national prominence. He was chosen by the Whigs in 1848 to be their candidate for vice president, paired with General Zachary Taylor.

ELECTION OF 1848. By 1846, the Texas issue had erupted into war with Mexico. Taylor, a slaveholding Louisiana planter, became a national hero by leading U.S. forces to victory. Texas would be a slaveholding state. But what of the vast new territories from New Mexico to California? These gains made the slavery issue compelling. Would slavery be allowed in them or not? Debate over the failed Wilmot Proviso of 1846, which would have banned slavery in all the territories won in the Mexican War, created great bitterness between North and South.

Both parties courted Taylor as a potential presidential candidate, and the Whigs finally succeeded. Millard Fillmore ran as the vice presidential candidate. While Taylor's candidacy ensured Whig victory in 1848, abolitionists regarded his selection as surrender to proslavery forces. Indeed, during the election Fillmore denied accusations of abolitionism. He stated that he regarded slavery as an evil, but believed that

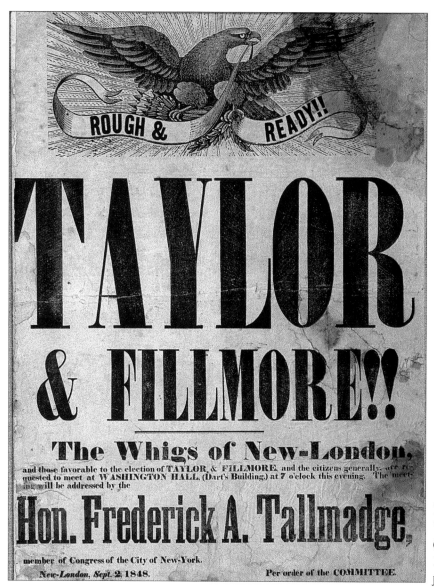

This is a broadside (poster) for a Whig rally in New London, Connecticut in the campaign of 1848. (Courtesy Collection of David J. and Janice L. Frent.)

"With the possible exception of Lyndon B. Johnson, Millard Fillmore may have been America's most unhappy vice-president. He and Abigail had never liked Washington and were always homesick for friends and the familiar surroundings of Buffalo. During his final term in Congress, he had finished second in the balloting for Speaker and had won universal praise for his work as chairman of the powerful committee on Ways and Means. If he had so desired, Buffalo would have given him a lifetime career of distinction in the House, or his well-earned reputation in the House would probably have made him a senator with even greater opportunities for influence and fame. With no taste for either, he had twice resigned to return home at the end of a term in Congress. He had not sought the vice-presidential nomination, but he had worked much harder than Taylor had for the election of his party's presidential ticket. "

• *Elbert B. Smith,* The Presidencies of Zachary Taylor & Millard Fillmore.

This portrait of Millard Fillmore appeared in Mathew Brady's Gallery of Illustrious Americans, *published in 1850. The book contained 24 portraits and sold for $20.*
(Courtesy Library of Congress.)

the issue was outside the domain of Congress and should be decided by individual states. While this position soothed Southern Whigs, it set Fillmore at odds with abolitionists in his party.

Support for war hero Taylor was irresistible, sweeping the Whigs into power once again. But in choosing Taylor the Whigs had bowed to the Southern wing of the party. While many Whigs remained antislavery, the party had lost the faith of hardcore abolitionists. However, it was the Southern wing that was surprised when Taylor's policies towards the new territories, especially California, proved distinctly antislavery.

Taylor's determination to hurry the territories into "free" statehood enraged Southerners. Texas laid claim to New Mexico and threatened to invade. A Texan attack on New Mexico could throw the nation into civil war. As the crisis built toward a climax, President Taylor died suddenly on 9 July 1850.

FIRST ANNUAL MESSAGE

. . . It was hardly to have been expected that the series of measures passed at your last session with the view of healing the sectional differences which has sprung from the slavery and territorial questions should at once have realized their beneficent purpose. All mutual concession in the nature of a compromise must necessarily be unwelcome to men of extreme opinions. And though without such concessions our Constitution could not have been formed, and cannot be permanently sustained, yet we have seen them made the subject of bitter controversy in both sections of the republic. It required many months of discussion and deliberation to secure the concurrence of a majority of Congress in their favor. It would be strange if they had been received with immediate approbation by people and states prejudiced and heated by the exciting controversies of their representatives. I believe those measures to have been required by the circumstances and condition of the country. I believe they were necessary to allay asperities and animosities that were rapidly alienating one section of the country from another and destroying those fraternal sentiments which are the strongest supports of the Constitution. They were adopted in the spirit of conciliation and for the purpose of conciliation. I believe that a great majority of our fellow citizens sympathize in that spirit and that purpose, and in the main approve and are prepared in all respect to sustain these enactments. I cannot doubt that the American people, bound together by kindred blood and common traditions, still cherish a paramount regard for the Union of their fathers, and that they are ready to rebuke any attempt to violate its integrity, to disturb the compromises on which it is based, or to resist the laws which have been enacted under its authority.

The series of measures to which I have alluded are regarded by me as a settlement in principle and substance—a final settlement of the dangerous and exciting subjects which they embraced. Most of these subjects, indeed, are beyond your reach, as the legislation which disposed of them was in its character final and irrevocable. It may be presumed from the opposition which they all encountered that none of those measures was free from imperfections, but in their mutual dependence and connection they formed a system of compromise the most conciliatory and best for the entire country that could be obtained from conflicting sectional interests and opinions.

For this reason I recommend your adherence to the adjustment established by those measures until time and experience shall demonstrate the necessity of further legislation to guard against evasion or abuse.

By that adjustment we have been rescued from the wide and boundless agitation that surrounded us, and have a firm, distinct, and legal ground to rest upon. And the occasion, I trust, will justify me in exhorting my countrymen to rally upon and maintain that ground as the best, if not the only, means of restoring peace and quiet to the country and maintaining inviolate the integrity of the Union. . . .

• *The Compromise measures of 1850 were the outstanding domestic achievement of President Fillmore's administration. Although the abolitionists would have nothing to do with him because of his role in the Compromise of 1850, he placed the preservation of the Union above any specific settlement of the slavery question. Fillmore delivered this message on 2 December 1850.*

PRESIDENCY. For months, Vice President Fillmore had presided over the congressional debate on the fate of the territories, and he understood the situation well. It was the flashpoint for the entire slavery issue. Proslavery forces dreaded the prospect of being so outnumbered in Congress by "free" states that they would be unable to block antislavery legislation. Antislavery forces were equally fearful of the possibility of the proslavery bloc becoming so powerful that slavery would be indefinitely preserved and perhaps even extended into currently free territories and states. The slavery debate was not merely about morality. Both sides saw their economic, political, and cultural survival entangled in the issue. Fillmore believed that the fight over slavery that was nearing would destroy the Union.

Now, as president, Fillmore was in a position to act to save the nation. He believed that the only answer was to secure the compromise that Congress had been unsuccessfully debating for seven months. Perhaps this resolution would please no one, but if it could put to rest the fears of the more moderate members of each side, then that would suffice. Fillmore negotiated the Compromise of 1850 and signed its provisions into law, defusing tensions enough to delay the final confrontation over slavery for another decade.

The Compromise admitted California to the Union as a free state; allowed the territories of New Mexico and Utah to decide their free or slaveholding status by popular vote; prohibited the slave trade in the District of Columbia; settled Texas boundary claims; and passed a more severe fugitive slave law. Fillmore believed that slaveholders must be reassured that the Fugitive Slave Act would be vigorously enforced, but his use of federal power to ensure the return of runaway slaves enraged abolitionist Whigs. His commitment to this last provision was a deathblow to his political career.

FUGITIVE SLAVE ACT

"Congress, as part of the Compromise of 1850, enacted a new Fugitive Slave Act, which was an extension of the 1793 Act, not a replacement for it. It contained these novel features: owners and agents were authorized to seize alleged fugitives with or without legal process; certificates of rendition could be granted by federal commissioners as well as federal judges; any adult male could be drafted into a posse to assist in capture and rendition; obstruction of the act was punishable by a fine of $1,000; . . .

Residents of the free states objected vehemently to the new statute. Throughout the 1850s, dramatic rescues and recaptures of runaways provided real-life drama to accompany the sensational success of the serialized, book, and stage versions of *Uncle Tom's Cabin*, with its melodramatic runaway scene. Federal authorities and northern conservatives responded to abolitionist challenges and to rescues of fugitives by affirming the constitutionality of the 1850 Act . . . and by demanding that resistance to enforcement of the measure be prosecuted as treason. Two efforts at doing so, however, ended in inglorious failure for the prosecution. In general, however, the northern states attempted to comply with the statute, and most blacks seized as fugitives under the act were sent into slavery."

• *William M. Wiecek, "Fugitive Slavery," in* Encyclopedia of the American Constitution, *edited by Leonard W. Levy, Kenneth L. Karst, and Dennis J. Mahoney.*

This poster for Millard Fillmore as the American (Know-Nothing) candidate shows typical patriotic symbols. (Courtesy Library of Congress.)

With the slavery issue seemingly put to rest, Fillmore sought to turn the nation's attention to fundamental Whig economic issues. He repeatedly emphasized that peace was good for prosperity, and expanding industry and commerce seemed to support that contention. Overseas trade thrived, and now, with the addition of California to the Union, Americans focused increasingly on the Pacific.

Great Britain had long been the United States's main trading rival in the Pacific. After the British forced open the China market in the Opium Wars of the early 1840s, it became clear to Whigs like Fillmore that British ambitions needed to be countered by establishment of new markets in Asia for U.S. trade. To promote this goal, the Fillmore administration, in 1852, sent a naval squadron under the command of Commodore Matthew Perry to China, Korea, and Japan.

The crowning achievement of Fillmore's foreign policy was the "opening" of Japan by Perry. For over two hundred years the Japanese had closed themselves off from the West. Of immediate interest to the United States was the use of Japan as a coaling station on the routes to China. But the trade possibilities were enormous. When, despite Japanese protests, Perry's squadron steamed relentlessly up the Bay of Yedo to the Japanese capital, Japanese isolation was over.

But by then, so was the presidency of Millard Fillmore. Although Southern Whigs tried to prevail upon him to run for reelection in 1852, Fillmore retired from office. Abolitionist Northern Whigs who were prepared to work against him were not sorry to see him go. The regional divisions within the party were beginning to shatter it. By 1856, a new abolitionist party, the Republicans, would spring from the Northern branch of the Whigs. Fillmore was the last Whig president.

Fillmore had one last hurrah, as the presidential candidate of the nativist American (Know-Nothing) Party in 1856, a movement dedicated to preventing "foreign" influence and preserving national unity at any cost. But the issues that would lead to the Civil War were unstoppable. Fillmore was soundly defeated. He spent his last 18 years involved in local issues in New York State, and died peacefully in Buffalo on 8 March 1874.

Millard Fillmore was nominated by the American (Know-Nothing) Party for the presidency in 1856. The vice presidential candidate was Andrew Jackson Donelson from Tennessee. Donelson was President Andrew Jackson's nephew and had been closely associated with Jackson for many years. Fillmore endorsed all the anti-foreign and anti-Catholic beliefs of the Know-Nothing Party. He came in a very distant third to Democrat James Buchanan and Republican John C. Frémont.

This is a silk ribbon for Fillmore and Donelson with a Know-Nothing Party slogan. (Courtesy Collection of David J. and Janice L. Frent.)

"Millard Fillmore, however, did not really want another term. He enjoyed the affluence, the acclaim, the comfort, and the satisfaction of having achieved his country's highest honor, but he had no thirst for power. He felt no great vindictiveness toward his enemies and had no real taste for unpleasant responsibilities and difficult choices that pitted his personal feelings against political exigencies. He later remembered that he had resolved not to seek election almost as soon as he actually had become president. He did not shrink from responsibilities, however, and no fair judge would call him a weakling. He served throughout his term with complete dedication and considerable ability, but by December 1851, his mind was made up. On that date, he confided to a long-time adherent that he would not be a candidate to succeed himself.

All available evidence indicates that this was an honest decision and not an effort to court a draft. Fillmore was not given to idle words."

• Elbert B. Smith, The Presidencies of Zachary Taylor & Millard Fillmore.

THE CABINET

SECRETARY OF STATE
John M. Clayton, 1850
Daniel Webster, 1850
Edward Everett, 1852

SECRETARY OF WAR
George W. Crawford, 1850
Charles M. Conrad, 1850

SECRETARY OF THE TREASURY
William M. Meredith, 1850
Thomas Corwin, 1850

POSTMASTER GENERAL
Nathan K. Hall, 1850
Samuel D. Hubbard, 1852

ATTORNEY GENERAL
John J. Crittenden, 1850

SECRETARY OF THE NAVY
William A. Graham, 1850
John P. Kennedy, 1852

SECRETARY OF THE INTERIOR
Thomas M. T. McKennan, 1850
Alexander H. H. Stuart, 1850

(Courtesy National Archives.)

William A. Graham (1804–1875). Graham was appointed secretary of the navy by President Millard Fillmore in 1850. He had previously served as governor of North Carolina (1845–1849).

As secretary of the navy, Graham reorganized the personnel of the navy and promoted exploration of the Amazon River. He also supported Commodore Matthew C. Perry's naval expedition to Japan (1852–1854).

In 1852, Graham became the Whig nominee for vice president on the ticket headed by General Winfield Scott. Four years later, he supported Millard Fillmore's campaign for president on the Know-Nothing (American) Party ticket.

In 1860, Graham strongly opposed secession from the Union, but when the Civil War began, he supported the South and served as a member of the Confederate Senate.

FAMILY

CHRONOLOGICAL EVENTS

13 March 1798	Abigail Powers born	30 March 1853	Abigail Fillmore died
21 October 1813	Caroline Carmichael born	26 July 1854	Daughter, Mary Abigail, died
5 February 1826	Abigail Powers married Millard Fillmore	10 February 1858	Caroline Carmichael McIntosh married Millard Fillmore
25 April 1828	Son, Millard Powers, born	8 March 1874	Millard Fillmore died
27 March 1832	Daughter, Mary Abigail (Abbie), born	11 August 1881	Caroline Fillmore died

(Courtesy Library of Congress.)

◄ Abigail Powers met Millard Fillmore when she was 20 years old and he was 19. She was a teacher, and he was her oldest student. They married eight years later. She continued to teach after their marriage, and she had a lifetime interest in education. As First Lady, she was shocked to learn that there were no books in the White House. At her urging, Congress gave her $5,000 to build a library.

She caught a cold at Franklin Pierce's Inauguration and it turned into pneumonia. She died several weeks later at the Willard Hotel in Washington. She and President Fillmore had already moved out of the White House.

Five years later, Fillmore married Caroline Carmichael McIntosh, a wealthy widow.

Mary Abigail Fillmore shared her mother's interest in education and taught briefly before her parents moved to Washington. She played several musical instruments and performed regularly for White House visitors. Abbie also acted as hostess because her mother was frequently ill.

A little more than a year after her mother's death, Abbie died of cholera while visiting her grandparents. She was 22 years old. ►

(Courtesy Library of Congress.)

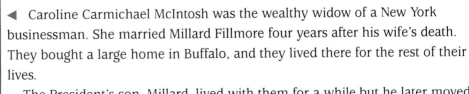

◄ Caroline Carmichael McIntosh was the wealthy widow of a New York businessman. She married Millard Fillmore four years after his wife's death. They bought a large home in Buffalo, and they lived there for the rest of their lives.

The President's son, Millard, lived with them for a while but he later moved. Before his own death at 61, he destroyed all his father's letters and journals. His own will directed his executors to destroy all his personal correspondence.

(Courtesy Library of Congress.)

MILLARD FILLMORE LOG CABIN BIRTHPLACE

Fillmore Glen State Park • Moravia, New York 13118 • Tel: (315) 497-0130

Located in Fillmore Glen State Park, approximately 30 miles southwest of Syracuse. Can be reached via Interstate 38. No fixed hours and no admission fee for the cabin. A fee is charged for vehicles entering the park.

The Millard Fillmore Log Cabin is a replica of the original cabin believed to have been built between 1795 and 1797. (Original drawing by Vincent Robert Evans.)

Millard Fillmore was born on 7 January 1800 in a log cabin a few miles east of Moravia in Locke Township, Cayuga County, New York. The cabin was torn down in 1852, but a replica based on the standard style for the period was dedicated in 1965. The replica measures 21 feet by 16 feet and has a single floor, a loft, three windows, and two doors. All the ironwork (locks, hinges, and latches) were hand-forged by the blacksmith at Colonial Williamsburg. It is furnished with period pieces (1800–1830) donated by local residents.

THE MILLARD FILLMORE HOUSE

24 Shearer Avenue • East Aurora, New York 14052 • Tel: (716) 652-8875

Located approximately 15 miles southeast of Buffalo. Open June through mid-October on Wednesday, Saturday and Sunday from 2 P.M. to 4 P.M. Special hours for groups by appointment only. For more information, write: Aurora Historical Society, Box 472, East Aurora, NY 14052. Owned, maintained, and staffed by volunteers from the Aurora Historical Society, Inc.

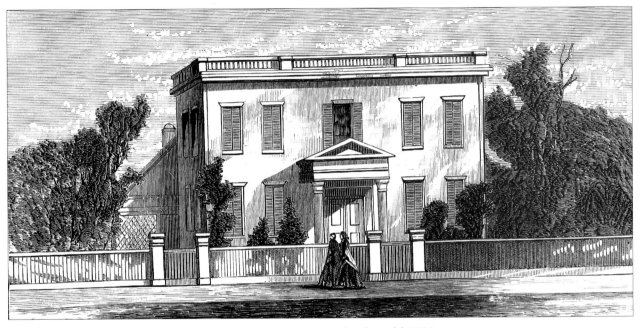

▲ *This old engraving shows the Fillmore home as it was in the mid-1800s.* (Courtesy Library of Congress.)

Millard Fillmore moved to Aurora, now East Aurora, in 1826. He married Abigail Powers, and they moved into a home across from his law office on Main Street. They lived there from 1819 to 1830. The house stood in disrepair until 1930, when it was purchased by artist Margaret Price (of Fisher-Price Toys), who had become interested in the house and its history. She had the structure moved to its present location and had it remodeled for her studio. In 1975, the house was purchased by the Aurora Historical Society and was restored to its original 1826 condition.

Millard Fillmore died in Buffalo, New York and was buried there at Forest Lawn Cemetery. (Courtesy Library of Congress.) ▶

Franklin Pierce

14TH PRESIDENT
OF THE UNITED STATES OF AMERICA

CHRONOLOGICAL EVENTS

23 November 1804	Born, Hillsborough, New Hampshire
1 September 1824	Graduated from Bowdoin College, Brunswick, Maine
5 September 1827	Admitted to bar, Hillsboro, New Hampshire
1829	Elected to New Hampshire State Legislature; served four terms
1831	Elected Speaker of New Hampshire state legislature
1833	Elected to U.S. House of Representatives
1836	Elected to U.S. Senate
16 February 1842	Resigned from U.S. Senate
1844	Appointed U.S. district attorney for New Hampshire
May 1846	Enlisted in U.S. Army
15 February 1847	Promoted to colonel
3 March 1847	Promoted to brigadier general
2 November 1852	Elected president
4 March 1853	Inaugurated president
July 1853	Authorized Gadsden Purchase
30 May 1854	Signed Kansas-Nebraska Act
1856	Lost nomination for reelection as president
8 October 1869	Died, Concord, Massachusetts

BIOGRAPHY

EARLY CAREER. Franklin Pierce, the fourteenth president of the United States, was born on 23 November 1804 in Hillsborough, New Hampshire. His father was Benjamin Pierce, a Revolutionary War general who would later be twice elected governor of New Hampshire. The elder Pierce was a prominent Democrat, and Franklin followed in his father's footsteps.

Graduating from Bowdoin College in 1824, Franklin Pierce was admitted to the bar in 1827. He was elected to the New Hampshire state legislature in 1829, when his father's second term as governor began. Four years later, he was elected to the U.S.

House of Representatives. He spent two terms in the House and was elected to the U.S. Senate in 1836, where he remained until he resigned in 1842.

This resignation was Pierce's first stumble on the political path that seemed set for him. While he was handsome and charming, he was aware of his limitations as a politician. Always loyal to the party, he was never a leader, and he often felt outclassed by the giants of his day—men like John C. Calhoun, Henry Clay, and Daniel Webster. An important factor in his decision to leave public office was his wife's disapproval. Mrs. Pierce hated public life, hated politics, and hated the social circuit that her

Franklin Pierce was chosen as the Democratic candidate for the presidency, in 1852, on the 49th ballot. Senator William Rufus King of Alabama was then chosen as the vice presidential candidate. They easily defeated the Whig candidates, Winfield Scott and William A. Graham. (Courtesy Collection of David J. and Janice L. Frent.)

husband fit into so well. Possibly she recognized that he fit too well in this world—politics was lubricated with hard liquor, and Pierce was an alcoholic.

RETURN TO PUBLIC LIFE. Pierce seemed more

suited to a military life. In college he had commanded a company of militia composed of his classmates. When the Mexican War began, he left his law practice and his work in local New

INAUGURAL ADDRESS

My Countrymen: It is a relief to feel that no heart but my own can know the personal regret and bitter sorrow over which I have been borne to a position so suitable for others rather than desirable for myself. . . .

In expressing briefly my views upon an important subject which has recently agitated the nation to almost a fearful degree, I am moved by no other impulse than a most earnest desire for the perpetuation of that Union which has made us what we are. . . . The sentiments I now announce were not unknown before the expression of the voice which called me here. My own position upon this subject was clear and unequivocal, upon the record of my words and my acts, and it is only recurred to at this time because silence might perhaps be misconstrued. . . . From that radiant constellation which both illumines our own way and points out to struggling nations their course, let but a single star be lost, and, if these be not utter darkness, the luster of the whole is dimmed. Do my countrymen need any assurance that such a catastrophe is not to overtake them while I possess the power to stay it? It is with me an earnest and vital belief that as the Union has been the source, under Providence, of our prosperity to this time, so it is the surest pledge of a continuance of the blessings we have enjoyed, and which we are sacredly bound to transmit undiminished to our children. The field of calm and free discussion in our country is open, and will always be so, but never has been and never can be traversed for good in a spirit of sectionalism and uncharitableness. The founders of the Republic dealt with things as they were presented to them, in a spirit of self-sacrificing patriotism, and, as time has proved, with a comprehensive wisdom which it will always be safe for us to consult. Every measure tending to strengthen the fraternal feelings of all the members of our Union has had my heartfelt approbation. To every theory of society or government, whether the offspring of feverish ambition or of morbid enthusiasm, calculated to dissolve the bonds of law and affection which unite us, I shall interpose a ready and stern resistance. I believe that involuntary servitude, as it exists in different states of this confederacy, is recognized by the Constitution. I believe that it stands like any other admitted right, and that the states where it exists are entitled to efficient remedies to enforce the constitutional provisions. I hold that the laws of 1850, commonly called the "compromise measures," are strictly constitutional and to be unhesitatingly carried into effect. I believe that the constituted authorities of this Republic are bound to regard the rights of the South in this respect as they would view any other legal and constitutional right, and that the laws to enforce them should be respected and obeyed, not with a reluctance encouraged by abstract opinions as to their propriety in a different state of society, but cheerfully and according to the decisions of the tribunal to which their exposition belongs. Such have been, and are, my convictions, and upon them I shall act. I fervently hope that the question is at rest, and that no sectional or ambitious or fanatical excitement may again threaten the durability of our institutions or obscure the light of our prosperity. . . .

• *The Compromise of 1850 dominated the 1852 presidential campaign. The Democrats deadlocked as the leading contenders—Stephen A. Douglas and James Buchanan—could not obtain the then two-thirds necessary for nomination. On the 49th ballot, a "dark horse," Franklin Pierce, former senator from New Hampshire, received the party's endorsement. Pierce's solid Democratic victory over General Winfield Scott signaled the break-up of the faction-ridden Whig Party.*

The new President delivered his inaugural address (4 March 1853) without a manuscript or notes. Pierce's son had died two months before so inaugural festivities were curtailed. It is this grief that the President refers to in the first sentence of his speech.

Hampshire politics to lead a brigade of volunteers. While military glory eluded Brigadier General Pierce, he was well respected for his service.

Pierce's political moment came in 1852. When the incumbent Whig President Millard Fillmore declined to run for reelection, he left behind a party torn by division over slavery. The split in the Whig Party offered the Democrats a great opportunity, but the many prominent Democrats bidding for nomination canceled each other out, deadlocking the Democratic national convention. On the 49th ballot the Democrats finally settled on a "dark horse" compromise candidate—Franklin Pierce.

Right from the start of his presidency, Pierce was overwhelmed by the job. Weeks before Pierce's inauguration, he and his wife celebrated by taking their eleven-year-old son, Bennie, on a train ride that ended in an accident. Bennie was the only

A PROCLAMATION

Whereas information has been received by me that sundry persons, citizens of the United States and others resident therein, are preparing, within the jurisdiction of the same, to enlist, or enter themselves, or to hire or retain others to participate in military operations within the State of Nicaragua:

Now, therefore, I, Franklin Pierce, President of the United States, do warn all persons against connecting themselves with any such enterprise or undertaking, as being contrary to their duty as good citizens and to the laws of their country and threatening to the peace of the United States.

I do further admonish all persons who may depart from the United States, either singly or in numbers, organized or unorganized, for any such purpose, that they will thereby cease to be entitled to the protection of this Government.

I exhort all good citizens to discountenance and prevent any such disreputable and criminal undertaking as aforesaid, charging all officers, civil and military, having lawful power in the premises, to exercise the same for the purpose of maintaining the authority and enforcing the laws of the United States.

In testimony whereof I have hereunto set my hand and caused the seal of the United States to be affixed to these presents.

Done at the city of Washington, the 8th day of December, 1855, and of the Independence of the United States the eightieth:

FRANKLIN PIERCE

• *William Walker, an American adventurer, with a small group of Mexican War veterans and unemployed men seeking excitement, took sides in a civil war in Nicaragua. Walker set up a government and made himself commander in chief of the army in 1855. John Wheeler, the U.S. minister to Nicaragua, gave recognition to Walker's government and assured Walker of the support of the United States. Southern expansionists regarded Walker's actions as an opportunity to extend slavery further south.*

However, Secretary of State William Marcy convinced President Pierce that Walker was just a troublemaker. Walker sent a representative to Washington who tried to recruit men for their army. At Marcy's urging, Pierce issued a proclamation against such activity on 8 December 1855.

By April 1856, Pierce changed his mind. He felt that recognizing Walker's government would give him a better chance of getting southern support. Walker took over the presidency himself and tried to reopen the international slave trade. He was soon thrown out of the country.

(Courtesy National Archives.)

"The 1850s were a time that would have tested severely even the most creative and assertive leadership. Pierce lacked such qualities, and he did not grow into the job. No President was more handsome or presidential in appearance than Franklin Pierce, and fewer were less qualified for the office." Larry Gara, "Pierce, Franklin," Encyclopedia of the American Presidency, *edited by Leonard W. Levy and Louis Fisher.*

35

passenger killed. Mrs. Pierce blamed her husband's presidential victory for the loss of her son, especially when she learned that, contrary to his denials, Pierce had sought the nomination. When the Pierces entered the White House, Mrs. Pierce locked herself in her bedroom and did not leave there often for the next four years.

THE PIERCE PRESIDENCY. Stunned and grief-stricken, the new president took office to face problems and issues that would have discouraged a far more capable man. The fires of abolitionism burned more and more strongly in the North, while Southerners hardened in their determination to resist any antislavery legislation. While the Compromise of 1850 had raised hopes that the issue might be laid to rest, by 1852 it was clear that such hopes were in vain.

The question of statehood loomed for the territories of Kansas and Nebraska, and Southerners in Congress pressed for the repeal of the Missouri Compromise of 1820, which restricted slavery to territories south of the Mason-Dixon line. At mid-century there was strong pressure to allow the new states to decide by popular vote whether they would be free or slaveholding.

Pierce was a "doughface," a proslavery Northerner. When Congress passed the Kansas-Nebraska Act in 1854, which would open to popular vote the question of the "free" or "slaveholding" status of those territories, he signed it into law. Proslavery settlers and abolitionists poured into Kansas to try to swing the vote in favor of their respective positions. Very quickly the area erupted into open warfare between the two opposing sides, giving the territory the name "Bleeding Kansas." Pierce made no attempt to ensure fair elections, and he blamed the violence on radical abolitionists.

SEEKING NEW TERRITORIES. Pierce's policies continued to favor slavery. The ongoing goal of the proslavery side was to acquire new slaveholding territories. To this end, proslavery supporters had sought for years to add Cuba to the United States. This huge Caribbean island was one of the last great holdings of the Spanish Empire. Several million slaves worked Cuba's sugar industry. These slaves represented both a threat and a promise to U.S. slaveholders. If they gained their freedom, they might inspire U.S. slaves to revolt, but if Cuba became a U.S. slave territory or state it would vastly increase the voting power of congressional slave-holding interests. The Pierce administration was humiliated when a communication regarding secret negotiations with Great Britain and France was leaked to the public. The Ostend Manifesto, as the communication was called, raised the fury of abolitionists, particularly since it advocated using military force if the Spanish refused to sell the island.

PRESIDENTIAL ACCOMPLISHMENTS. Pierce's administration encouraged the development of rail transportation and in 1853 bought a tract of land along the Mexican border, known as the Gadsden Purchase, to aid the development of a southern route across the continent. Pierce approved of the mission to Japan by Commodore Matthew Perry, begun by the Fillmore administration. Pierce's administration also negotiated the Canadian Reciprocity Treaty in 1854, which granted the United States fishing privileges in Canadian waters, and attempted to acquire the Hawaiian islands and gain naval bases in Santo Domingo.

Pierce sought reelection at the end of his term but was denied the nomination by the Democratic Party in favor of James Buchanan. He retired to his home in New Hampshire and avoided public service from then on. During the Civil War, he favored preservation of the Union but disapproved of Lincoln's determination to win unconditional victory over the Confederacy.

Pierce died on 8 October 1869. He had been a weak, ineffective president. While the divisions in the nation when he took office were probably too great to have been resolved in any way other than by war, his actions contributed to the deepening of the crisis, rather than helping to find solutions that might have preserved the Union and satisfied the conflicting needs of the opposing sides.

VICE PRESIDENT

William Rufus de Vane King
(1786–1853)

CHRONOLOGICAL EVENTS

1786	Born, Sampson County, North Carolina, 7 April
1801	Attended University of North Carolina at Chapel Hill
1807	Elected to North Carolina State House of Commons
1810	Elected to U.S. House of Representatives
1822	Elected to U.S. Senate
1844	Appointed U.S. minister to France
1852	Elected vice president
1853	Died, near Selma, Alabama, 18 April

BIOGRAPHY

A quiet peacemaker, William R. King stood apart from the impassioned orators of his era. Born in North Carolina, King was the son of a wealthy slave-owning planter. He attended the University of North Carolina and became a lawyer. After serving in the North Carolina legislature, he won election to the U.S. House of Representatives just as he turned the minimum age of 25. Following the War of 1812, King left Congress to go abroad on diplomatic missions for the United States. While in Europe, he contracted tuberculosis.

Returning to the United States, King moved from North Carolina to the Alabama frontier. There he purchased land for a plantation he called King's Bend. He helped write Alabama's state constitution and became one of the state's first U.S. senators. In the Senate, King joined Democrats in support of President Andrew Jackson and in opposition to Henry Clay's Whigs.

In Washington, the unmarried King shared living quarters with another bachelor, Senator James Buchanan of Pennsylvania, and became acquainted with many Northern Democrats. Recognized as a southern moderate, he was considered for vice president in 1840. Mentioned again in 1844, King instead accepted appointment to serve as U.S. minister to France. In 1848, he was appointed to fill a vacancy in the Senate.

King reentered a Senate deeply divided over the issue of slavery in the territories. He worked diligently to preserve order and to achieve a compromise between North and South. Zachary Taylor's death in 1850 made Millard Fillmore president and created a vacancy in the vice presidency. The Senate elected King president pro tempore of the Senate to preside in the absence of a vice president. He won acclaim for his efforts to maintain order during the heated debates. In 1852, Franklin Pierce defeated James Buchanan for the Democratic nomination for president. In order to appease Buchanan's supporters, the delegates selected King for vice president. During the campaign, however, King's tuberculosis worsened. After the Democrats won, he traveled to Cuba to recuperate. His rapidly declining health prevented his return to Washington for the inauguration, and Congress permitted him to take his oath in Cuba. A month later he came back to King's Bend, where he died, never able to occupy the office to which he had so long aspired.

THE CABINET

SECRETARY OF STATE
William L. Marcy, 1853

SECRETARY OF WAR
Jefferson Davis, 1853

SECRETARY OF THE TREASURY
James Guthrie, 1853

POSTMASTER GENERAL
James Campbell, 1853

ATTORNEY GENERAL
Caleb Cushing, 1853

SECRETARY OF THE NAVY
James C. Dobbin, 1853

SECRETARY OF THE INTERIOR
Robert McClelland, 1853

(Courtesy Architect of the Capitol.)

Jefferson Davis (1808–1889). Davis was appointed secretary of war by President Franklin Pierce in 1853. He had commanded the Mississippi Rifles in the Mexican War and was wounded at Buena Vista (1847). He returned as a hero and was presented with a sword of honor by the Mississippi legislature, which chose him as U.S. senator (1847–1851).

As secretary of war, Davis supported plans for a southwestern transcontinental railway and supervised the surveys for the route. He modernized the army by introducing new infantry tactics and the use of iron gun carriages instead of wood. He also experimented with using camels in the military to transport men and supplies in the southwest.

Davis returned to the Senate in 1857. He advocated southern rights and the importance of state sovereignty within the Union. In a resignation speech to the Senate on 21 January 1861, he justified secession.

On 18 February 1861, he was inaugurated at Montgomery, Alabama as provisional president of the Confederate Government and was then elected for a six-year term and inaugurated at Richmond, Virginia (22 February 1862). In his inaugural address, Davis stated: "We have entered upon the career of independence, and it must be inflexibly pursued."

On 10 May 1865, he was captured by Union forces at Irwinville, Georgia. Davis was charged with treason and imprisoned at Fort Monroe. In May 1867, he was released on bail. He was never brought to trial.

After traveling abroad, Davis spent the last years of his life writing his account of the war, *Rise and Fall of the Confederate Government* (1881).

FAMILY

CHRONOLOGICAL EVENTS

12 March 1806	Jane Means Appleton born	6 January 1853	Son, Bennie, died
19 November 1834	Jane Means Appleton married Franklin Pierce	2 December 1863	Jane Pierce died
13 April 1841	Son, Benjamin (Bennie), born	8 October 1869	Franklin Pierce died

Jane Means Appleton married Franklin Pierce in her grandparents' home in Amherst, New Hampshire. They lost one son in infancy and another died at the age of four. Jane Pierce blamed the latter death on their life in Washington, where her husband was a member of Congress. Less than a year after Bennie was born, Pierce resigned from the U.S. Senate. They returned to Concord, New Hampshire where he practiced law. When the National Democratic Convention of 1852 chose Pierce as their candidate, his wife became angry and upset.

Two months before his Inauguration, their surviving son, Bennie, was killed in a tragic accident. The railroad car in which they were traveling rolled down an embankment. The only fatality was Bennie, 11 years old.

Jane Pierce never recovered from Bennie's death. She became more depressed, and she spent almost two years in virtual seclusion in the upstairs living quarters at the White House. She did not make her first public appearance until New Year's Day in 1855. After Pierce lost his bid for renomination, they traveled extensively in Europe. She died of tuberculosis and was buried in Concord, New Hampshire.

(Courtesy of Library of Congress.)

FRANKLIN PIERCE HOMESTEAD

Route 31 • Hillsborough, New Hampshire 03244 • Tel: (603) 464-5858

Franklin Pierces's father, Benjamin, operated the homestead as a tavern until he purchased a 200-acre site which became a working farm. The home was painted on only three sides to save money. After 20 years or more, the back was painted red. (Courtesy Library of Congress.)

Located approximately 18 miles southwest of Concord. Can be reached via Route 9: Turn north onto Route 31; second house on the right. Open daily July and August from 10 A.M. to 4 P.M.; Sunday from 1 P.M. to 4 P.M. June, and September through Columbus Day, open Saturday and Sunday only from 1 P.M. to 4 P.M. Additional open days: Memorial Day weekend, 4 July and 5 September. Admission fee. Tours available for groups by special arrangement; call: (603) 464-4260. Maintained by the Hillsborough Historical Society.

Franklin Pierce's father, Benjamin, a Revolutionary War veteran, settled in Hillsborough in 1786. He purchased land on what is now the site of Lake Pierce. The Pierce Homestead was built in 1804, the same year that President Pierce was born. It contained 10 spacious rooms, hand-stenciled walls, and imported wallpaper. During Pierce's youth, the homestead was the gathering place of the great men of the state and nation, which later helped boost his political career.

The homestead was purchased by the State of New Hampshire in 1930. The site was then leased to the Hillsborough Historical Society. In 1953, a restoration project was initiated under the direction of Russel Tobey of the New Hampshire Parks and Recreation Department. The gardens surrounding the home, along with the artificial pond and the summer house, were restored at that time.

THE PIERCE MANSE

14 Penacook Street
P.O. Box 425
Concord, New Hampshire 03302-0425
Tel: (603) 224-9620

The Pierce Manse is located in Concord, New Hampshire. The word "manse" in its earliest usage designated "the house occupied by the householder." It is applied to this house to differentiate it from other homes connected with President Pierce. (Courtesy Library of Congress.) ▶

Located approximately 15 miles north of Manchester. Open mid-June through Labor Day, Monday to Friday, from 11 A.M. to 3 P.M. Closed on holidays. Special hours by appointment only. Admission fee, with special rates available for groups. Groups of 10 or more admitted by advance notice only; call: (603) 224-7668 or (603) 224-0094. Owned and maintained by the Pierce Brigade, a nonprofit organization dedicated to historic preservation.

The Pierce Manse was the Pierce family home from 1842 to 1848. When Franklin Pierce purchased this house, he had just resigned from the U.S. Senate to resume his law practice. In 1846, he enlisted in the army and served in the Mexican War. His wife, Jane, and son, Benjamin, went to stay with relatives and did not return until after the war in 1848. At that time, Pierce sold the house.

In 1966, the house was threatened with demolition by an urban-renewal project. The Pierce Brigade was formed to save the house, and they moved it to its present location in Concord's Historic District. A replica of the original barn and shed were added in 1993. The house has been restored to resemble, as much as possible, what it looked like when the Pierces lived there. Many of the present furnishings belonged to President Pierce and other family members.

Franklin Pierce died on 8 October 1869 at his home in Concord, New Hampshire. He was buried next to his wife, Jane, at Old North Cemetery in Concord.
(Courtesy Library of Congress.)

James Buchanan

15TH PRESIDENT
OF THE UNITED STATES OF AMERICA

CHRONOLOGICAL EVENTS

23 April 1791	Born, Cove Gap, near Mercersburg, Pennsylvania
27 September 1809	Graduated from Dickinson College, Carlisle, Pennsylvania
17 November 1812	Admitted to bar, Lancaster, Pennsylvania
1814	Elected to Pennsylvania House of Representatives
1820	Elected to U.S. House of Representatives
1832	Appointed U.S. minister to Russia
6 December 1834	Elected to U.S. Senate
1843	Reelected to U.S. Senate
1845	Appointed secretary of state
1852	Appointed U.S. minister to Great Britain
4 November 1856	Elected president
4 March 1857	Inaugurated president
6 March 1857	*Dred Scott v. Sanford* decision
24 August 1857	Panic of 1857 began
2 February 1858	Submitted Lecompton constitution to Congress; recommended Kansas be admitted as a slave state
October 1859	John Brown's Raid, Harpers Ferry, Virginia (now West Virginia)
1 June 1868	Died at Wheatland, Lancaster, Pennsylvania

BIOGRAPHY

EARLY CAREER. James Buchanan, the fifteenth president of the United States, was born on 23 April 1791 near Mercersburg, Pennsylvania. His parents were farmers in rural Pennsylvania. After Buchanan graduated from Dickinson College in 1809, he studied law for three years and was admitted to the bar in 1812. Personable and successful, he soon moved into politics, entering the Pennsylvania legislature in 1814 as a Federalist. He was elected to the U.S. House of Representatives in 1820. He switched to the Democratic Party in 1828 after the collapse of the Federalist Party.

Buchanan remained in Congress until 1831. He made friends mostly with Southerners in Congress and embraced their ideal of the graceful agrarian life. Wheatland, his estate in Pennsylvania, resembled the large Southern plantations. A lifelong bachelor, Buchanan supervised his large extended family of nieces and nephews, many of whom were orphans in his care.

Buchanan's political views were shaped by his experience and friendships. In keeping with the Jacksonian ideals of the Democratic Party, he strongly opposed homestead grants, land grants for schools, high tariffs, and government-sponsored development of roads, harbors, and canals. He also sympathized with Southern plantation owners; while he occasionally admitted to believing that slavery was a bad thing, he never strongly opposed the South's "peculiar institution."

NATIONAL PROMINENCE. In 1832, Buchanan was appointed U.S. minister to Russia. Two years later, he entered the U.S. Senate, where he remained for 11 years. Appointed secretary of state by President James K. Polk in 1845, he supported the annexation of Texas, helped settle the Oregon border dispute with Great Britain, extended the Monroe Doctrine, and made attempts to purchase Cuba from Spain. His tendency on the important issues of his day was always to seek a middle position, but his actions in regard to slavery invariably supported the Southern position.

He was convinced that slavery was guaranteed by the Constitution and saw abolitionists as a threat to the stability of the Union.

In 1852, President Franklin Pierce appointed Buchanan U.S. minister to Great Britain. In 1854, Buchanan co-authored the Ostend Manifesto (see Pierce biography), a secret agreement among the United States, Great Britain, and France that supported the purchase of Cuba by the United States and justified seizure of Cuba by force if Spain refused to sell. This agreement pleased U.S. slave owners, who worried that if the Spanish freed their Cuban slaves or those slaves successfully rebelled, slaves in the United States would be inspired to revolt as well. While Buchanan's role in drafting the Manifesto angered abolitionists, his

JAMES BUCHANAN,
DEMOCRATIC CANDIDATE FOR PRESIDENT OF THE UNITED STATES.

James Buchanan and John C. Breckinridge were the Democratic candidates for the presidency and vice presidency in the 1856 election. (Courtesy Library of Congress.)

Col. JOHN C. FREMONT,
REPUBLICAN CANDIDATE FOR PRESIDENT OF THE UNITED STATES.

James Buchanan easily defeated John C. Frémont, the Republican candidate for the presidency, in the 1856 election. Frémont was an army officer, U.S. senator, and a daring explorer. His expedition to California and Oregon in 1843, with Kit Carson as his guide, gave him a national reputation. (Courtesy Library of Congress.)

absences from the country meant that he could avoid taking a stance on the Kansas-Nebraska issue. While the nation argued over the free or slaveholding status of those territories, and while other politicians became clearly identified with one side of the issue or the other, Buchanan could present himself as a moderate when he ran for president on the Democratic ticket in 1856. He won the election easily against his opponents, the radical Republican John C. Frémont and former President Millard Fillmore, who was the candidate of the anti-immigrant Know-Nothing Party.

BUCHANAN'S PRESIDENCY. Buchanan became president as the nation came closer to civil war over the slavery issue. He would be the last presi-

dent with the opportunity to seek a compromise that would prevent war, and his great failure was his inability to find that compromise. Instead, he pursued policies that sought to satisfy the South but that instead left both pro and antislavery forces confused and angry about what each felt was a threat to its way of life.

Only two days after his inauguration and thus before Buchanan could take any measures to deal with the coming crisis, the Supreme Court decided the Dred Scott case. Declaring the Missouri Compromise unconstitutional and preventing territorial governments from prohibiting slavery, this decision opened all the territories to slave interests. Free-Soilers and abolitionists alike were

Dred Scott was involved in one of the most famous decisions of the United States Supreme Court: Dred Scott v. Sandford. (Courtesy Library of Congress.)

"Scott was a Missouri slave owned by an army medical officer named John Emerson, who took him to live at military posts in Illinois and in federal territory north of 36° 30' where slavery had been prohibited by the Missouri Compromise. In 1846, Scott brought suit against Emerson's widow in St. Louis, claiming that he had been emancipated by his residence on free soil. Missouri precedent was on his side, and after two trials he won his freedom. In 1852, however, the state supreme court reversed that judgment. By a 2–1 vote and in bitterly sectional language, it declared that the state would no longer enforce the antislavery law of other jurisdictions against Missouri's own citizens. Scott's residence elsewhere, it held, did not change his status as a slave in Missouri. . . . "

• *Don E. Fehrenbacher, "Dred Scott v. Sandford,"* Encyclopedia of the American Constitution, *edited by Leonard W. Levy, Kenneth L. Karst, and Dennis J. Mahoney.*

angered by the decision.

Meanwhile, in Kansas, proslavery leaders convened a constitutional convention in the town of Lecompton in which Free-Soilers refused to participate. When this congress drafted a proslavery constitution, Buchanan endorsed it, ignoring the protests even of Robert J. Walker, the Kansas territorial governor, whom Buchanan himself had appointed. Buchanan's acceptance of a proslavery Kansas brought him into direct conflict with Senator Stephen A. Douglas of Illinois, the most dynamic member of the Democratic Party. This caused a split within the party. A congressional coalition of Republicans and Northern Democrats led by Douglas rejected the Lecompton constitution.

As tensions over slavery continued to build, Buchanan's attempts to pacify the South by upholding the Fugitive Slave Law and preventing abolitionist agitation further infuriated anti-slavery forces. In strongholds of abolition, like Massachusetts, there was open talk of secession from the Union. But when secession came, it was the Southern states that broke away.

John Brown's raid at Harpers Ferry, Virginia in October 1859 heightened Southern fear of abolitionist violence, even though Brown's attempt to start a slave revolt was a hopeless failure. For Northerners, the subsequent execution of Brown provided a martyr and hero. As for the president, Buchanan held the North, and particularly the abolitionists, responsible for all the discord.

Buchanan had decided when he was elected not to run again, and the Democratic Party split its support in 1860. The Northern faction chose Stephen A. Douglas, while Southerners nominated John C. Breckinridge, Buchanan's vice president.

John Brown was a Kansas abolitionist who had murdered some of his proslavery neighbors. He and his followers marched into Harpers Ferry, Virginia, where there was an armory and an arsenal. He intended to start a slave uprising. He was captured by Robert E. Lee, found guilty of treason and murder, and was hanged. Speaking of slavery, Brown said that, "the crimes of this guilty land will never be purged away but with blood." (Courtesy National Archives.)

This split cleared the way for the victory of Abraham Lincoln, the Republican candidate. Convinced despite Lincoln's assurances that the power of the presidency would now be focused on the destruction of slavery, Southern states began to secede.

His critics insisted that Buchanan could have still prevented the collapse of the Union in the remaining months of his presidency, but he was helpless as events steamrollered toward the bloodbath of the Civil War. While he publicly supported the Union during the war, he still believed that a compromise with the South could have been reached and wrote his memoirs seeking to justify his position. He died on 1 June 1868 at his estate, Wheatland, in Lancaster, Pennsylvania.

FOURTH ANNUAL MESSAGE TO CONGRESS

Throughout the year since our last meeting, the country has been eminently prosperous in all its material interests. The general health has been excellent, our harvests have been abundant, and plenty smiles throughout the land. Our commerce and manufactures have been prosecuted with energy and industry, and have yielded fair and ample returns. In short, no nation in the tide of time has ever presented a spectacle of greater material prosperity than we have done, until within a very recent period.

Why is it, then, that discontent now so extensively prevails, and the Union of the states, which is the source of all these blessings is threatened with destruction?

The long continued and intemperate interference of the northern people with the question of slavery in the southern states has at length produced its natural effects. The different sections of the Union are now arrayed against each other, and the time has arrived, so much dreaded by the Father of his Country, when hostile geographical parties have been formed. . . .

And this brings me to observe, that the election of any one of our fellow citizens to the office of president does not of itself afford just cause for dissolving the Union . . . How, then, can the result justify a revolution to destroy this very Constitution? Reason, justice, a regard for the Constitution, all require that we shall wait for some overt and dangerous act on the part of the president elect, before resorting to such a remedy. It is said, however, that the antecedents of the president elect have been sufficient to justify the fears of the South that he will attempt to invade their constitutional rights. But are such apprehensions of contingent danger in the future sufficient to justify the immediate destruction of the noblest system of government ever devised by mortals? . . .

The Southern states, standing on the basis of the Constitution, have a right to demand this act of justice from the states of the North. Should it be refused, then the Constitution, to which all the states are parties, will have been wilfully violated by one portion of them in a provision essential to the domestic security and happiness of the remainder. In that event, the injured states, after having first used all peaceful and constitutional means to obtain redress, would be justified in revolutionary resistance to the government of the Union. . . .

• *After Lincoln's election in November 1860, Buchanan's administration began to fall apart. Edwin Stanton, appointed attorney general on 19 December 1860, recorded in his diary that Buchanan "lived through an agony of indecision." The President prepared his last annual message to Congress with great care. It contained a strong denial of the right of secession, but a confession of the federal government's helplessness in dealing with the actual secession of South Carolina.*

VICE PRESIDENT

John Cabell Breckinridge
(1821–1875)

CHRONOLOGICAL EVENTS

1821	Born, Lexington, Kentucky, 15 January
1839	Graduated from Centre College, Danville, Kentucky
1850	Elected to U.S. House of Representatives
1856	Elected vice president
1860	Ran unsuccessfully for president
1861	Elected to U.S. Senate
1861	Served in the Confederate army and as Confederate secretary of war
1875	Died, Lexington, Kentucky, 17 May

BIOGRAPHY

The U.S. vice president who led a Confederate assault on Washington, D.C. during the Civil War, John C. Breckinridge was born into a prominent Kentucky family. One of his grandfathers had been Thomas Jefferson's attorney general.

Breckinridge, who practiced law, volunteered to lead a Kentucky infantry regiment during the Mexican War. Returning a war hero, he was elected to the Kentucky State House of Representatives. A Jacksonian Democrat in the Whig leader Henry Clay's hometown of Lexington, Kentucky, Breckinridge won a seat in the U.S. House of Representatives in 1851. In Congress, he defended both the right of slavery in the Western territories and the Union.

In 1854, Illinois Senator Stephen A. Douglas introduced the Kansas-Nebraska Act. Breckinridge supported Douglas's policy of "popular sovereignty," which allowed settlers to decide whether to permit slavery in the territories. Rather than neutralize slavery as a national issue, however, the Kansas-Nebraska Act caused an angry public reaction that forged the new Republican Party.

Democrats chose James Buchanan over Stephen A. Douglas as their presidential candidate in 1856. Breckinridge nominated a Kentucky "favorite son" candidate for vice president. His nominating speech was so forceful that the convention nominated Breckinridge instead. Only 36 years old, he became the nation's youngest vice president.

Suspicious of Breckinridge's friendship with Douglas, President Buchanan ignored his vice president and rarely invited him to the White House. Yet when Douglas broke with Buchanan over bringing Kansas into the Union as a slave state, Vice President Breckinridge sided with Buchanan and shifted away from Douglas.

In 1860, the Democratic convention nominated Douglas for president. Southern Democrats bolted and formed a third party that nominated Breckinridge. Republicans chose Abraham Lincoln. By splitting the Democratic Party, Breckinridge ensured Lincoln's election.

After the Southern states seceded and the Civil War began, Breckinridge became a general in the Confederate army. Breckinridge commanded Confederate troops in many battles, including a July 1864 raid on Washington, D.C. When the Confederacy collapsed, Breckinridge fled abroad. He lived in exile until President Andrew Johnson pardoned him in 1868.

THE CABINET

SECRETARY OF STATE
Lewis Cass, 1857
Jeremiah S. Black, 1860

SECRETARY OF WAR
John B. Floyd, 1857
Joseph Holt, 1861

SECRETARY OF THE TREASURY
Howell Cobb, 1857
Philip F. Thomas, 1860
John A. Dix, 1861

POSTMASTER GENERAL
Aaron V. Brown, 1857
Joseph Holt, 1859
Horatio King, 1861

ATTORNEY GENERAL
Jeremiah S. Black, 1857
Edwin M. Stanton, 1860

SECRETARY OF THE NAVY
Isaac Toucey, 1857

SECRETARY OF THE INTERIOR
Jacob Thompson, 1857

(Courtesy Architect of the Capitol.)

Lewis Cass (1782–1866). Cass was appointed secretary of war by President Andrew Jackson in 1831. He had previously served as governor of Michigan Territory (1813–1831).

As secretary of war, Cass directed the Black Hawk War against the Sac and Fox Indians in the Wisconsin Territory (1832) and the Second Seminole War in Florida (1835–1842). He also supervised the tragic removal of Eastern Native Americans to trans-Mississippi lands.

In 1848, Cass won the Democratic presidential nomination but lost the election to General Zachary Taylor. During the campaign, Cass originated the idea of "popular sovereignty" which would permit the admission to the Union of territories with or without slavery.

Cass was appointed secretary of state by President James Buchanan in 1857. He resigned in 1860 to protest Buchanan's decision not to reinforce the federal forts in Charleston Harbor, South Carolina that were being threatened by secessionists.

FAMILY

James Buchanan was the only president to remain a bachelor. He became guardian to his niece, Harriet Lane, when she became an orphan at the age of nine. Buchanan supervised her upbringing and education. When President Franklin Pierce appointed him U.S. minister to Great Britain in 1852, he brought her to London with him.

She was then 23 years old and she was very successful as his hostess. When Buchanan was elected president in 1856, she joined him in the White House where she was also a gracious and charming hostess. Her youthful energy was a welcome relief after the sadness of the Pierce years.

Her wedding was at Buchanan's home, Wheatland, in 1866, when she was 36 years old. She gave birth to two sons who did not live to adulthood. She died in 1903 and left most of her money to a children's wing at Johns Hopkins University. She asked that it be dedicated to the memory of her sons.

(Courtesy Library of Congress.)

JAMES BUCHANAN CABIN

Mercersburg Academy • Mercersburg, Pennsylvania 17236 • Tel: (717) 328-2151

Located on the grounds of the Mercersburg Academy, approximately 17 miles southwest of Chambersburg. Open by appointment. Admission is free. Preserved and maintained by the Mercersburg Academy.

In 1865, President Buchanan wrote of his birthplace: "It is a rugged but romantic spot, and the mountain and mountain stream under the scenery captivating. I have warm attachments for it . . ."
(Courtesy The Mercersburg Academy.)

James Buchanan, Sr. arrived in Philadelphia in 1783 and became a clerk at Tom's Trading Post in Cove Gap (then called Laribee's Gap). Five years later he bought the trading post and married Elizabeth Speer. They renamed the trading post Stony Batter after the Buchanan family homestead in Northern Ireland. The future president lived there with his parents and two sisters from his birth in 1791 until 1796, when the family moved to Mercersburg.

In 1834, the birthplace cabin was moved to South Fayette Street in Mercersburg. At this time, another log structure was added to the north end of the cabin. In 1925, the cabin was dismantled and moved to North Second Street in Chambersburg by four local businessmen. It was used as a tourist attraction and gift shop until the spring of 1953 when the Mercersburg Academy purchased the cabin and moved it to their campus, where it stands today.

President Buchanan's niece, Harriet Lane Johnson, provided in her will for a monument to be erected in honor of her late uncle. The monument was completed in 1907, on the original site of the birthplace cabin. It stands 31 feet high and 38 feet square in a pyramid structure containing 50 tons of hammered American gray granite and 250 tons of native rubble and mortar.

WHEATLAND

1120 Marietta Avenue • Lancaster, Pennsylvania 17603 • Tel: (717) 392-8721

Located 1.5 miles west of Lancaster on Marietta Avenue (Route 23) near the intersection with President Avenue. Open daily April through November from 10 A.M. to 4:15 P.M. Closed Thanksgiving. Admission fee, with special rates for groups by appointment. Daily tours available. Special Victorian Christmas Candlelight Tours are held for one week in early December. Call the above number for exact dates and hours. Two gift shops and a snack bar are located on the premises. Tickets are sold in the carriage house located near the parking lot. Owned, operated and maintained by The James Buchanan Foundation, an educational, nonprofit organization.

Buchanan wrote his 1857 inaugural address in the library at Wheatland. He had great affection for the mansion and praised the "comforts and tranquillity of home as contrasted with the troubles, perplexities, and difficulties" of public life. (Original drawing by Vincent Robert Evans.)

Wheatland was built in 1828 by William Jenkins, a wealthy lawyer and banker. In 1848, Buchanan purchased the 22-acre estate while serving as secretary of state in President James K. Polk's cabinet. Eight years later, he campaigned for the presidency from the mansion's front porch and held political meetings in the library during the months before his election. Buchanan retired to Wheatland in 1861 and lived there until his death in 1868.

The 17-room, Federal-style brick mansion has been restored to the condition it was in during the years of Buchanan's occupancy. The estate is now situated on four acres of land. Victorian and Empire furnishings are on display in the mansion. The site also contains the original outer buildings—the smokehouse, the privy, and the carriage house. Guides dressed in period costumes are available to answer questions and to conduct tours inside the mansion.

Abraham Lincoln

16TH PRESIDENT
OF THE UNITED STATES OF AMERICA

CHRONOLOGICAL EVENTS

12 February 1809	Born, near Hodgenville, Harlin County (now Larue County), Kentucky
1816	Moved with family to Indiana
1830	Moved with family to Illinois
1832	Served as a volunteer in the Black Hawk War
7 May 1833	Appointed postmaster for New Salem, Illinois
4 August 1834	Elected to Illinois state legislature, served four terms
9 September 1836	Admitted to bar, Springfield, Illinois
3 August 1846	Elected to U.S. House of Representatives
8 February 1855	Defeated for election to U.S. Senate
1858	Debated Stephen A. Douglas during senatorial campaign
5 January 1859	Deafeated for election to U.S. Senate
6 November 1860	Elected president
4 March 1861	Inaugurated president
13 April 1861	Surrender of Fort Sumter, South Carolina
15 April 1861	Issued proclamation to states for 75,000 militia
19 April 1861	Ordered blockade of the South
4 July 1861	Sent war message to Congress
20 May 1862	Signed Homestead Act
2 July 1862	Signed Morrill Act
22 September 1862	Issued preliminary Emancipation Proclamation
1 January 1863	Issued Emancipation Proclamation
3 March 1863	Signed Judiciary Act
4 July 1863	Surrender of Vicksburg, Mississippi
19 November 1863	Delivered Gettysburg Address
9 March 1864	Named Ulysses S. Grant general in chief of the Union army
28 June 1864	Fugitive Slave Act of 1850 repealed
30 June 1864	Signed Internal Revenue Act
4 July 1864	Vetoed Wade-Davis Reconstruction bill
8 November 1864	Reelected president
4 March 1865	Inaugurated president
9 April 1865	Confederate General Robert E. Lee surrendered at Appomattox, Virginia
14 April 1865	Shot by John Wilkes Booth
15 April 1865	Died, Washington, D.C.

BIOGRAPHY

To many people, Abraham Lincoln ranks as the greatest American president. More books have been written about him than about any other American.

There are several reasons for Lincoln's popularity. One reason is that he rose from obscurity to achieve great success. He was born in a log cabin in Kentucky on 12 February 1809 and grew up in frontier areas of Indiana and Illinois where schools were crude and basic and books were few. His parents could neither read nor write. Yet he managed to educate himself and to succeed as a lawyer.

Lincoln also remains popular because of his personality. He was tall, awkward, and not handsome, but he nevertheless made an unforgettable impression. Sometimes he was moody, but his face lit up when he talked, especially when he told a funny story. He always remained "Honest Abe," natural and unpretentious.

Another reason Lincoln is well remembered is the time when he was president. The years 1861 to 1865 were the years of the Civil War, a war that started shortly after Lincoln's election. The war resulted in the preservation of the Union and the emancipation of the slaves. After leading the Union throughout the war, Lincoln was assassinated at the very moment of victory. His death made him seem like a martyr who had sacrificed his life for Union and freedom.

However, the main reasons for Lincoln's enduring reputation are his actual achievements as president. He did not merely preside over the Civil War; he, more than any other one person, determined its outcome. As a politician, he gained and held leadership so that he was able to act as a statesman. As a statesman, he kept the North committed to the war aims of reunion and, later, emancipation. As a military leader, he took responsibility for the overall direction of the armed forces, a direction that led to victory. As a writer and speaker, he gave meaning to the war through his powerful and persuasive expression of democratic ideals.

John Hay was one of President Abraham Lincoln's two secretaries. His diary gives the first record of a famous saying: "The president tonight (23 December 1863) had a dream: He was in a party of plain people, and as it became known who he was, they began to comment on his appearance. One of them said, 'He is a very common-looking man.' The president replied, 'The Lord prefers common-looking people. That is the reason he makes so many of them.'"

This portrait of Abraham Lincoln was made on 27 February 1860. On that day, Lincoln gave the speech at the Cooper Union in New York that convinced many that Lincoln was the best presidential candidate the Republicans could offer. (Courtesy Library of Congress.)

EARLY POLITICAL CAREER. Until he ran for president, Lincoln had not seemed like an especially skillful politician. Certainly, he had not been a very successful one, although he was ambitious enough. "His ambition was a little engine that knew no rest," according to his law partner William H. Herndon. He was elected to several terms in the Illinois state legislature and served one term in the U.S. House of Representatives.

While in the House of Representatives, from 1847 to 1849, Lincoln gave much of his attention to the presidential election of 1848. As a member of the Whig Party, he tried to discredit the Democratic president, James K. Polk, and accused President Polk of deliberately provoking Mexico into war with the United States. In the presidential election of 1848, Lincoln and his fellow Whigs campaigned for Zachary Taylor, a general who had become a hero in the Mexican War. After Taylor won the election, Lincoln was badly disappointed by Taylor's failure to appoint him to a government office. He had counted on a reward from Taylor for his help in the presidential campaign and wanted to be named commissioner of the general land office.

Lincoln again became active in politics in 1854 when Congress passed the Kansas-Nebraska Act. According to this act, the settlers of Kansas and Nebraska could decide for themselves whether to permit slavery in those territories. The bill was largely the work of Stephen A. Douglas, a Democratic senator from Illinois. In allowing the people to choose for themselves whether to permit slavery in the two territories, the law

A HOUSE DIVIDED

If we could first know where we are, and whither we are tending, we could better judge what to do, and how to do it.

We are now far into the fifth year, since a policy was initiated, with the avowed object, and confident promise, of putting an end to slavery agitation.

Under the operation of that policy, that agitation has not only not ceased, but has constantly augmented.

In my opinion, it will not cease, until a crisis shall have been reached, and passed—

"A house divided against itself cannot stand."

I believe this government cannot endure, permanently half slave and half free.

I do not expect the Union to be dissolved—I do not expect the house to fall—but I do expect it will cease to be divided.

It will become all one thing, or all the other.

Either the opponents of slavery, will arrest the further spread of it, and place it where the public mind shall rest in the belief that it is in course of ultimate extinction; or its advocates will push it forward, till it shall become alike lawful in all the States, old as well as new—North as well as South. . . .

• *The Republican state convention met at the statehouse at Springfield, Illinois on 16 June 1858. They unanimously voted for Abraham Lincoln as their candidate to oppose Stephen A. Douglas in the upcoming contest for a U.S. Senate seat. David Herbert Donald, Lincoln's most recent biographer, notes that Lincoln gave his acceptance speech at eight o'clock that evening. He had memorized his speech and had no need to refer to notes. Donald says, "The 'house divided' quotation was one familiar to virtually everybody in a Bible-reading, churchgoing state like Illinois; it appeared in three of the Gospels."*

embodied the principle of popular sovereignty, or self-government, which Douglas supported.

Because the Kansas-Nebraska Act allowed Kansans and Nebraskans to vote to permit slavery in their territories, areas where Congress had previously prohibited it, the Act stirred up strong opposition among antislavery citizens in the Northern states. This "anti-Nebraska" movement led to the founding of a new political party, the Republican Party, which stood for "free soil," that is, for keeping slavery out of all the territories.

Lincoln joined the Republican Party and became one of its leaders in Illinois. Politics in that state became pretty much a contest between Lincoln and Douglas. Lincoln ran against Douglas for the U.S. Senate in 1858. In campaign speeches and in a series of joint debates, he called Douglas a proslavery conspirator and said that popular sovereignty was really a way of spreading slavery. Douglas, in turn, accused Lincoln of being an abolitionist. Actually, Lincoln did not favor immediate abolition, but he argued that "free soil" would lead to eventual abolition. Slavery could not survive, he said, if it could not expand. Although Lincoln lost the Senate race, he became well known. His reputation helped him to win the presidency.

ELECTION OF 1860. As the Republican presidential candidate in 1860, Lincoln planned his own campaign. His idea was to concentrate on the one issue— "free soil"—on which practically all Republican voters could agree. He did not campaign for himself because it was not yet considered proper for him to do so. However, he gave advice to those who campaigned for him. He instructed them to say nothing about other issues, such as the tariff, temperance, the rights of immigrants, or any other subject on which Republicans might be divided. This strategy worked. With the

Stephen A. Douglas defeated Abraham Lincoln for the U.S. Senate seat from Illinois in 1859. Douglas lost the presidential election of 1860 to Lincoln. He died of typhoid fever on 3 June 1861. (Courtesy Library of Congress.)

Democratic Party split between Stephen A. Douglas and John C. Breckinridge, Lincoln managed to win a large majority of the electoral votes, although he received less than 40 percent of the popular vote.

PRESIDENCY. The Republicans were in the minority in Congress until the Southern states seceded and took the Southern Democrats with them. The Northern Democrats remained strong enough to gain additional seats in Congress in the midterm elections of 1862. The party was divided, however, between the War Democrats, who supported the war aim of reunion, and the Copperheads, who wanted an early peace. The Republicans also were divided; the Radicals demanded that the war continue until all the

This photograph by Mathew Brady was used for the engraving of the Lincoln head on the five-dollar bill. Lincoln's son, Robert, said that it was "the most satisfactory likeness of him."
(Courtesy Library of Congress.)

slaves were emancipated, while the Conservatives were willing to settle for reunion alone.

As president and party leader, Lincoln faced the task of holding the support of Republicans while gaining the cooperation of Democrats. He succeeded fairly well in doing this throughout his term in office, slightly more than four years. He did this partly by influencing public opinion. At a time when there was no radio or television, he could speak only to as many people as could gather in front of him, and he did so on only a few

occasions while president. To reach a larger public, he used the newspapers. He granted interviews, wrote letters to editors, and even composed a few editorials to be published anonymously.

Lincoln dealt more effectively with individuals in person than with the public in general. He had a gift for getting along with people, overcoming differences, and holding the support of men who disagreed with him and with one another. His humor helped him. Sometimes he told a funny story to ease a tense situation or to distract visitors

First Inaugural Address

. . . A disruption of the federal Union, heretofore only menaced, is now formidably attempted.

I hold that, in contemplation of universal law and of the Constitution, the Union of these states is perpetual. Perpetuity is implied, if not expressed, in the fundamental law of all national governments. It is safe to assert that no government proper ever had a provision in its organic law for its own termination. Continue to execute all the express provisions of our national Constitution, and the Union will endure forever, it being impossible to destroy it except by some action not provided for in the instrument itself.

Again: if the United States be not a government proper, but an association of states in the nature of contract merely, can it, as a contract, be peaceably unmade by less than all the parties who made it? One party to a contract may violate it—break it, so to speak—but does it not require all to lawfully rescind it?

Descending from these general principles, we find the proposition that in legal contemplation the Union is perpetual confirmed by the history of the Union itself. The Union is much older than the Constitution. It was formed, in fact, by the Articles of Association in 1774. It was matured and continued by the Declaration of Independence in 1776. It was further matured, and the faith of all the then thirteen states expressly plighted and engaged that it should be perpetual, by the Articles of Confederation in 1778. And finally, in 1787, one of the declared objects for ordaining and establishing the Constitution was "to form a more perfect Union."

But if destruction of the Union by one or by a part only of the states be lawfully possible, the Union is less perfect than before the Constitution, having lost the vital element of perpetuity.

It follows from these views that no state upon its own mere motion can lawfully get out of the Union; that resolves and ordinances to that effect are legally void, and that acts of violence within any state or states against the authority of the United States are insurrectionary or revolutionary, according to circumstances. . . .

Physically speaking, we cannot separate. We cannot remove our respective sections from each other nor build an impassable wall between them. A husband and wife may be divorced and go out of the presence and beyond the reach of each other, but the different parts of our country cannot do this. They cannot but remain face to face, and intercourse, either amicable or hostile, must continue between them. Is it possible, then, to make that intercourse more advantageous or more satisfactory after separation than before? Can aliens make treaties easier than friends can make laws? Can treaties be more faithfully enforced between aliens than laws can among friends? Suppose you go to war, you cannot fight always; and when, after much loss on both sides and no gain on either, you cease fighting, the identical old questions, as to terms of intercourse, are again upon you. . . .

In your hands, my dissatisfied fellow countrymen, and not in mine, is the momentous issue of civil war. The government will not assail you. You can have no conflict without being yourselves the aggressors. You have no oath registered in heaven to destroy the government, while I shall have the most solemn one to "preserve, protect, and defend it."

I am loath to close. We are not enemies, but friends. We must not be enemies. Though passion may have strained it must not break our bonds of affection. . . .

• *Abraham Lincoln was inaugurated on 4 March 1861. By this time, seven states had already seceded from the Union, and Jefferson Davis had been sworn in as the president of the Confederacy.*

Abraham Lincoln delivered his first Inaugural Address on 4 March 1861. (Courtesy National Archives.)

from complaints they had come to make. He used his winning ways most often on members of his cabinet, congressmen, governors, and others who themselves had political influence. Essentially, he was a "politician's politician."

To unify and strengthen the Republican Party, Lincoln made good use of the patronage system; that is, he appointed his supporters to government positions as a reward for helping his campaign. He also appointed to his cabinet all his former rivals for the presidential nomination. He appointed William H. Seward, a Conservative who had been his foremost rival, to serve as secretary of state and named Salmon P. Chase, a leading

Radical, secretary of the treasury. He managed to keep both men in the cabinet until 1864, when he accepted Chase's resignation from the Treasury Department. Lincoln delayed Chase's appointment as chief justice of the Supreme Court until after the election of 1864 to be sure of his support during the campaign.

ELECTION OF 1864. Lincoln masterminded his own campaign in 1864, as he had done in 1860. This time he engineered the nomination of Andrew Johnson of Tennessee, a Democrat and a Southerner, as his running mate to replace Hannibal Hamlin, a strong abolitionist. Thus he ran on a "Union" ticket, one that could appeal to

Second Inaugural Address

. . . Now, at the expiration of four years, during which public declarations have been constantly called forth on every point and phase of the great contest which still absorbs the attention and engrosses the energies of the nation, little that is new could be presented. The progress of our arms, upon which all else chiefly depends, is as well known to the public as to myself, and it is, I trust, reasonably satisfactory and encouraging to all. With high hope for the future, no prediction in regard to it is ventured.

On the occasion corresponding to this four years ago all thoughts were anxiously directed to an impending civil war. All dreaded it, all sought to avert it. While the inaugural address was being delivered from this place, devoted altogether to saving the Union without war, insurgent agents were in the city seeking to destroy it without war—seeking to dissolve the Union and divide effects by negotiation. Both parties deprecated war, but one of them would make war rather than let the nation survive, and the other would accept war rather than let it perish, and the war came.

One-eighth of the whole population were colored slaves, not distributed generally over the Union, but localized in the southern part of it. These slaves constituted a peculiar and powerful interest. All knew that this interest was somehow the cause of the war. To strengthen, perpetuate, and extend this interest was the object for which the insurgents would rend the Union even by war, while the government claimed no right to do more than to restrict the territorial enlargement of it. Neither party expected for the war the magnitude or the duration which it has already attained. Neither anticipated that the cause of the conflict might cease with or even before the conflict itself should cease. Each looked for an easier triumph, and a result less fundamental and astounding. Both read the same Bible and pray to the same God, and each invokes His aid against the other. It may seem strange that any men should dare to ask a just God's assistance in wringing their bread from the sweat of other men's faces, but let us judge not, that we be not judged. The prayers of both could not be answered. That of neither has been answered fully. The Almighty has His own purposes. "Woe unto the world because of offenses; for it must needs be that offenses come, but woe to that man by whom the offense cometh." If we shall suppose that American slavery is one of those offenses which, in the providence of God, must needs come, but which, having continued through His appointed time, He now wills to remove, and that He gives to both North and South this terrible war as the woe due to those by whom the offense came, shall we discern therein any departure from those divine attributes which the believers in a living God always ascribe to Him? Fondly do we hope, fervently do we pray, that this mighty scourge of war may speedily pass away. Yet, if God wills that it continue until all the wealth piled by the bondsman's 250 years of unrequited toil shall be sunk, and until every drop of blood drawn with the lash shall be paid by another drawn with the sword, as was said three thousand years ago, so still it must be said "the judgments of the Lord are true and righteous altogether."

With malice toward none, with charity for all, with firmness in the right as God gives us to see the right, let us strive on to finish the work we are in, to bind up the nation's wounds, to care for him who shall have borne the battle and for his widow and his orphan, to do all which may achieve and cherish a just and lasting peace among ourselves and with all nations.

• *When Abraham Lincoln was overwhelmingly reelected, the Union was winning the Civil War. General Robert E. Lee would surrender to General Ulysses S. Grant only a month after the inauguration.*

Democrats as well as Republicans. During the campaign he removed uncooperative jobholders, gave electioneering advice to party workers, and made arrangements for as many soldiers as possible (most of whom were Republicans) to vote. His Democratic opponent, the former U.S. Army General George B. McClellan, ran on a platform that declared the war a failure and criticized Lincoln for restricting civil liberties. Before election day, McClellan's attacks on the progress of the war were contradicted by news of great Union victories, especially the capture of Atlanta, Georgia. Lincoln won 55 percent of the popular vote and received 212 electoral votes to McClellan's 21.

If Lincoln had been merely a shrewd politician, he would have given us little cause to remember him. A great president must not only legitimately get power, he must also use that power for worthwhile public ends. Lincoln did both. Through his skill as a statesman, he was able to achieve much.

THE STATESMAN. A statesman seldom can choose between the perfectly good and the absolutely bad. Usually he faces alternatives that have desirable as well as undesirable aspects. And sometimes he must sacrifice one object in order to attain another that he values more. So it was with Lincoln.

By 1860, slavery had come to seem a terrible wrong to Lincoln, as it had to most Northerners. He once said he could not remember a time when he did not think of it that way. While he considered slavery "an evil not to be extended," he did not yet believe it could be immediately abolished. He still relied on the hope that slavery would eventually die out in the states where it already existed if it could be kept from spreading to new areas.

After the Civil War began, a growing number of Northerners demanded that the abolition of slavery be made a war aim. But Lincoln held back. He overruled two of his generals, John C. Frémont and David Hunter, when they proclaimed freedom for the slaves of disloyal masters in their respective military districts. Antislavery people found fault with him for being slow to act. In a letter to the powerful newspaper editor Horace Greeley, he explained that his "paramount object" was "to save the Union" and "not to save or destroy slavery." He added, however, that he had not given up his "personal wish that all men everywhere could be free."

There were several reasons why Lincoln delayed so long to act on his "personal wish." The Republican platform, on which he was elected, had promised that the party would not interfere with slavery in the Southern states. When inaugurated, Lincoln had taken an oath to abide by the Constitution, and at first he could find in the Constitution no power by which a president, or an army general, could declare the slaves free. Even if Lincoln as president had such power, he knew that he would offend many white people in the North if he used it. Northern whites feared that the slaves, once freed, would move north and compete with them for jobs. Slaveholders still loyal to the Union in the border states of Maryland, Missouri, and Kentucky might shift their support to the Confederacy. Then the war might be lost. If it were, Lincoln would be powerless either to save the Union or to emancipate the slaves.

With these considerations in mind, Lincoln made up an emancipation plan that he thought would stir up comparatively little opposition. Under his plan, slaveholders would be paid to free their slaves and would have to do so only gradually. The slaves, once freed, would be resettled in Africa or in other places outside the United States. Lincoln hoped that his program for gradual emancipation could begin immediately in the border states. But border-state politicians refused their support, and African American leaders objected to the "colonization" of former slaves outside this country, which was, after all, their home.

Lincoln issued his Emancipation Proclamation only after his plan for colonization of the freed slaves ran into resistance. It was issued in its preliminary form on 22 September 1862 and in its final form on 1 January 1863. Lincoln had finally decided he could take such a step as a war mea-

This engraving was made from a huge oil painting by Francis B. Carpenter that was finished in 1864. It shows President Lincoln reading the draft of the Emancipation Proclamation to members of his cabinet. Secretary of War Edwin M. Stanton is seated at the left, and Secretary of the Treasury Salmon P. Chase is standing between Stanton and the President. Secretary of State William H. Seward is seated in front of the table, and Secretary of the Navy Gideon Welles, Secretary of the Interior Caleb B. Smith, Postmaster General Montgomery Blair, and Attorney General Edward Bates are behind it. (Courtesy National Archives.)

sure—a means of strengthening the Union and weakening the Confederacy. He based his proclamation on his "war power" as commander in chief of the army and navy. That is why the proclamation declared free only those slaves in areas still in rebellion, omitting those in the loyal slave states and in those parts of the South already recovered by the Union armies. On the basis of the war power, Lincoln could act against only those slaveowners who were at war with the U.S. Government.

The proclamation also stated that henceforth the freed slaves would be "received into the armed service of the United States to garrison forts, positions, stations and other places, and to man vessels of all sorts in said service." Now the army began eagerly to recruit African Americans, free and slave, North and South. By the end of the war, approximately 200,000 African Americans had served as Union soldiers. They were a great help in achieving victory for the Union.

Lincoln was not sure whether his proclamation would bring lasting freedom to many of the nearly 4 million slaves in the South. To do this, a constitutional amendment would be necessary. Lincoln helped persuade Congress to pass the Thirteenth Amendment, which abolished slavery. He was glad to see the amendment ratified by Illinois and then by other states, but he did not live to celebrate its final adoption late in 1865.

When abolition became a war measure, it also became a war aim. At the start of the war, in 1861,

Lincoln's peace terms as well as his war aims could have been expressed in a single word—reunion. If the process of reunion was quick and easy, he seemed to think, the rebels might be encouraged to lay down their arms. When they continued to resist, his terms became somewhat more difficult.

Late in 1863, he proposed his "10 percent plan" for the reconstruction of the seceded states and the reconstruction of the Union. By then, the states of Louisiana, Tennessee, and Arkansas had been substantially reconquered. According to the plan, any of these three states could apply for readmission to the Union when 10 percent of the existing voters had taken an oath of future loyalty and adopted a constitution rejecting secession and abolishing slavery. Radicals in Congress thought that Lincoln's plan did not go nearly far enough. They demanded that the rights to vote and to hold office be taken away from leading Confederates and given to the freed slaves.

At the end of the war, Lincoln still believed, as he had believed all along, that the war's main objective should be to restore the "seceded states, so-called," to their "proper practical relations" with the Union. He hoped that these states would discover some way by which whites and blacks "could gradually live themselves out of their old relations to each other, and both come out better prepared for the new." He also urged the states to provide education for the freed people and to give the vote to some of the men— "as, for instance, the very intelligent, and especially those who fought gallantly in our ranks." It is impossible to know what changes he might have made in his views on reconstruction if he had lived.

War aims and peace plans occupied a great deal of Lincoln's attention, because they were not only basic but controversial issues. Important matters of economic policy also came before him. However, these required less of his time and care because he had fewer differences with his fellow Republicans in Congress and with the country regarding them. "The legitimate object of govern-ment," he once said, "is to do for a community of people whatever they need to have done, but cannot do at all, or cannot do so well for themselves, in their separate and individual capacities." In his earlier days, as a Whig, he had favored that party's program of encouraging business and developing resources by means of a national bank, a protec-tive tariff, and federal expenditures for improving transportation. As president, he favored a similar program, which the Republicans had inherited from the Whigs. During the war, Congress passed and Lincoln signed bills establishing a national banking system, raising the tariff, and providing aid for the construction of a "transcontinental" railroad.

As a rule, Lincoln left the details of finance to his secretary of the treasury and the details of for-eign affairs to his secretary of state. But he carefully supervised and sometimes overruled his department heads. Early in his administration, he had to show who was boss when Secretary of State William H. Seward proposed to Lincoln that he take charge of the government. Seward pro-posed to overcome disunion and avoid a civil war by provoking a foreign war. Lincoln made it plain to Seward and to all others in the cabinet that he, not any of them, was chief executive.

THE MILITARY LEADER. As commander in chief of the army and the navy, Lincoln used his authority not only to issue the Emancipation Proclamation but also to give overall direction to the conduct of military operations. At first, he was not well prepared for doing so. He had no military personal experience except for brief service in the Black Hawk War (1831–1832), during which he saw no "live, fighting Indians" but had "a good many bloody struggles with the mosquitoes," as he afterward joked. As president, he studied mili-tary textbooks and sought advice from army officers. He soon discovered, however, that he could not depend on the experts, who did not always agree among themselves. He would have to make his own decisions.

Lincoln's first big decision had to do with Fort Sumter, in Charleston Harbor, South Carolina. At the time of his inauguration, U.S. troops still held Fort Sumter. They were running short of supplies and were threatened by Confederates, who claimed the fort and surrounded it. His top military adviser, General in Chief Winfield Scott, recommended that he withdraw the troops. Instead, Lincoln sent a relief expedition, after first notifying the Confederates. Without waiting for the expedition to arrive, they opened fire on the fort on 12 April 1861. Thus they made themselves the aggressors, as far as most Northerners were concerned.

Lincoln's second important decision was to proclaim a blockade of the Southern ports. This was his own idea, rather than the suggestion of any of his generals or admirals. As the navy acquired more and more ships, the blockade became increasingly tight. It helped to bring about the eventual defeat of the Confederates by depriving them of essential imports, such as medicine and most manufactured goods, including guns.

In his next crucial decision, Lincoln hit upon the idea of advancing his armies on several fronts at once. Again he disagreed with General Scott, who favored concentrating on a movement down the Mississippi River. Instead, Lincoln ordered an advance from Washington toward the Confederate capital of Richmond, Virginia. This advance resulted in the Union defeat at Bull Run on 21 July 1861. For the next several days he thought about the lessons to be learned from this defeat. "I state my general idea of this war to be," he then wrote to one of his generals, "that we have the greater numbers, and the enemy has the greater facility of concentrating forces upon points of collision; that we must fail, unless we can find some way of making our advantage an overmatch for his; and that this can only be done by menacing him with superior forces at different points, at the same time."

Lincoln had hit on the right basic idea. He now needed a general in chief who would see that it was carried out. He tried a succession of army commanders—George B. McClellan, John Pope, Ambrose E. Burnside, Joseph Hooker, George Gordon Meade—but was disappointed with each of them in turn. Finally, in March 1864, he put Ulysses S. Grant in charge of all the Union armies. Grant, together with his generals, William T. Sherman, Philip Sheridan, and George H. Thomas, succeeded in carrying to a victorious conclusion Lincoln's strategy of advancing on several fronts at once.

Besides his strategic planning, Lincoln contributed to military success in another significant way. He helped with the development of the tools of war. Inventors kept thinking up new kinds of arms and ammunition. Some of them were promising, and others useless or worse than useless, being dangerous to the user. The promising ones needed to be sorted out, tested, further developed, and perhaps adopted. Lincoln took responsibility for much of this work. When inventors came to him with models and samples, he arranged for demonstrations and tests, sometimes firing an experimental gun himself. He then recommended to army and navy ordinance officials the adoption of the inventions that he had approved. Thus he contributed to the wartime progress in military technology—the development and introduction of explosive bullets, incendiary shells (causing fire), mortars, repeating rifles, and even machine guns.

THE ADVOCATE OF DEMOCRACY. "Our popular government has often been called an experiment," Lincoln said in 1861. "Two points in it, our people have already settled—the successful establishing, and the successful administering of it. One still remains—its successful maintenance against a formidable attempt to overthrow it."

The maintenance of the Union was the central issue of the Civil War, as Lincoln saw it. From time to time he rephrased the issue, elaborated on it, and put it in words of increasing eloquence. He also had to deal with the matter as a practical problem in the day-to-day use of his presidential powers. This meant facing a persistent dilemma: he was trying to maintain a popular government, that is, a democracy, and so he hesitated to use other

In October 1862, General George McClellan had allowed General Robert E. Lee and his army to cross the Potomac River. President Lincoln had ordered McClellan to pursue Lee's army, but McClellan had not done so. Lincoln went to Virginia to meet with McClellan and to review the troops. Soon after, Lincoln fired McClellan and put Ambrose E. Burnside in charge of the Army of the Potomac.

While on this trip, Lincoln was photographed with Allan Pinkerton, chief of the secret service (left), and Major General John A. McClernand (right). (Courtesy Library of Congress.)

than democratic means. However, democratic means seemed hardly adequate for the emergencies that he continually faced.

After the war had begun, he called Congress to meet in a special session, but he waited for nearly three months. During that time he took on his own a number of steps that required congressional authorization, such as enlarging the army. He also suspended the writ of habeas corpus, which helps protect citizens from unlawful detention by the authorities. Lincoln's critics said that only Congress could authorize the suspension of habeas corpus. Lincoln defended his move by saying that his purpose was to help the authorities arrest suspected traitors and hold them without trial. Without the suspension of habeas corpus the war might have been lost at the very beginning. There were many Confederate sympathizers and outright secessionists in Maryland, and some of them were destroying railroad tracks and telegraph lines between Washington and Baltimore. In Baltimore a mob attacked a regiment of Massachusetts troops on their way to Washington. Some Maryland legislators planned to hold a secession convention in the state. Lincoln could be sure of maintaining communications between Washington and the North and of holding the capital itself only by taking prompt and decisive action to deal with such threats. When Congress met, it approved what he had done.

On later occasions, with the backing of Congress, the army arrested and held people without allowing them a trial. The best known person arrested was Clement L. Vallandigham, an Ohio Democrat. In and out of Congress, Vallandigham opposed the war and the draft, which he insisted was unconstitutional. The seizure of such an important politician proved embarrassing to Lincoln, but he dared not let Vallandigham go free. "Must I shoot a simple-minded soldier boy who deserts," he asked, "while I must not touch a hair of the wily agitator who induces him to desert?" Yet he did not wish to make a martyr of Vallandigham by holding him a prisoner. Lincoln

handled this problem by banishing the "wily agitator" behind the Confederate lines.

In a few instances Lincoln allowed his generals to shut down unfriendly newspapers, but not for long. He stated his policy in these instructions to an army officer: "You will only arrest individuals and suppress assemblies or newspapers when they may be working palpable [evident] injury to the military in your charge, and in no other case will you interfere with the expression of opinion in any form or allow it to be interfered with by others. In this you have a discretion to exercise with great caution, calmness, and forbearance."

Political opponents and the opposition press continually criticized Lincoln as a dictator, but he was nothing of the sort. He did not have the slightest inclination toward dictatorship. In words as well as deeds, he devoted himself to the ideal of self-government, which he considered at stake in the Civil War. "And this issue embraces more than the fate of these United States," he once declared. "It forces us to ask: 'Is there, in all republics, this inherent and fatal weakness? Must a government, of necessity, be too strong for the liberties of its own people, or too weak to maintain its own existence?'"

Surely this is the fundamental difficulty confronting all democratic governments—the difficulty of reconciling liberty and authority, accomodating the rights of the individual and the welfare of the group. Lincoln was not a political theoretician or philosopher. He did not write long articles on methods of dealing with this difficulty. But he accurately viewed it as the essential issue of the war and thus helped to give the war the broad significance it deserved.

LINCOLN'S DEATH. John Wilkes Booth, born to a slaveholding family in Maryland, was a famous and highly successful actor. Booth favored independence for the South and opposed freedom for the slaves. At first, he plotted to kidnap Lincoln and exchange him for Confederate prisoners. To help him carry out the plot, he enlisted a number of Confederate sympathizers and spies. Then, when the Confederacy lost the war, he decided to

GETTYSBURG ADDRESS

Four score and seven years ago our fathers brought forth on this continent, a new nation, conceived in liberty, and dedicated to the proposition that all men are created equal.

Now we are engaged in a great civil war, testing whether that nation or any nation so conceived and so dedicated, can long endure. We are met on a great battlefield of that war. We have come to dedicate a portion of that field, as a final resting place for those who here gave their lives that that nation might live. It is altogether fitting and proper that we should do this.

But, in a larger sense, we can not dedicate—we can not consecrate—we can not hallow—this ground. The brave men, living and dead, who struggled here, have consecrated it, far above our poor power to add or detract. The world will little note, nor long remember what we say here, but it can never forget what they did here. It is for us the living, rather, to be dedicated here to the unfinished work which they who fought here have thus far so nobly advanced. It is rather for us to be here dedicated to the great task remaining before us—that from these honored dead we take increased devotion to that cause for which they gave the last full measure of devotion—that we here highly resolve that these dead shall not have died in vain—that this nation, under God, shall have a new birth of freedom—and that government of the people, by the people, for the people, shall not perish from the earth.

• *President Lincoln stated his commitment to democracy in the final words of the Gettysburg Address. On 19 November 1863, Edward Everett, president of Harvard and distinguished public figure, was the major speaker at the dedication. A crowd of some 20,000 listened to Everett speak for two hours. Then President Lincoln delivered his immortal words.*

John Wilkes Booth. (Courtesy National Archives.)

kill Lincoln. Booth shot the President in Ford's Theatre on the night of 14 April 1865, Lincoln, only 56 years old, died the next day. Booth, his leg broken when he jumped from the theater boxes on to the stage, fled on horseback to Virginia. There he was shot to death in a barn after it was surrounded and set on fire.

Lincoln's body lay in the East Room of the White House on 19 April. It was carried to the Capitol Rotunda later that day, and it laid in state there until the evening of 20 April. Almost 4,000 people per hour filed past the coffin. At 8 A.M. the next morning the nine-car funeral train carrying Lincoln's coffin pulled out of Washington. Also on board was the coffin of the President's son, Willie, who had died in 1862. At 9 A.M. on 3 May, the train arrived in Springfield, Illinois, Lincoln's final resting place.

◄ *Mathew Brady made a photograph of the box at Ford's Theatre in which Lincoln met his death. Secretary of War Stanton ordered the photographic plate destroyed. The order was carried out, but not before a print was made.* (Courtesy National Archives.)

A military tribunal presided over by General David Hunter tried the conspirators in President Lincoln's assassination. Four were hanged in the yard of the Washington Penitentiary. Mathew Brady received permission to photograph the execution. The four were: Mrs. Mary Suratt, the owner of the boarding house where John Wilkes Booth and the other conspirators met; George Atzerodt who was supposed to kill Vice President Andrew Johnson but lost his nerve; David Herold who went with Booth to the barn where Booth was killed; and Lewis Powell, who tried to kill Secretary of State William H. Seward. (Courtesy Library of Congress.) ▼

VICE PRESIDENT

**Hannibal Hamlin
(1809–1891)**

CHRONOLOGICAL EVENTS

1809	Born, Paris Hill, Maine, 27 August
1836	Elected to Maine State House of Representatives
1842	Elected to U.S. House of Representatives
1848	Elected to U.S. Senate
1860	Elected vice president
1865	Appointed collector of the Port of Boston
1869	Again elected to U.S. Senate
1881	Appointed U.S. minister to Spain
1891	Died, Bangor, Maine, 4 July

BIOGRAPHY

The first Republican vice president, Hannibal Hamlin, spent most of his political career as a Democrat. A doctor's son, Hamlin grew up in a prosperous Maine family. Studying law with an abolitionist lawyer converted him to the antislavery cause.

Sociable and politically ambitious, Hamlin was elected to the Maine House of Representatives. There he led the fight to abolish capital punishment in the state. He went on to serve in the U.S. House of Representatives, where he joined other antislavery members in promoting the Wilmot Proviso, which banned slavery in territories taken during the Mexican War.

Elected to the U.S. Senate, Hamlin opposed the Compromise of 1850 because it permitted the spread of slavery. He was one of only four Democratic senators to vote against the Kansas-Nebraska Act of 1854. In 1856, Republicans persuaded Hamlin to head their ticket by running for governor. He agreed only if the legislature would quickly send him back to the Senate. Hamlin served less than two months as governor before returning to the Senate.

Republicans nominated Hamlin to run with Abraham Lincoln in 1860, expecting him to appeal to antislavery Democrats. Stunned by the unexpected nomination to a job he considered "a fifth wheel on a coach," Hamlin regretted having to leave the Senate. After their election, President Lincoln consulted Hamlin on patronage but otherwise sent him to the sidelines of his administration. During the Civil War, Vice President Hamlin sympathized with congressional radicals and joined them in pressing Lincoln to issue an emancipation proclamation.

Since Lincoln considered Hamlin expendable, he remained neutral in 1864 when Republicans dropped the vice president in favor of Andrew Johnson, the wartime governor of Tennessee. That summer, Vice President Hamlin briefly served as a private in the Maine Coast Guard. Following Lincoln's assassination, President Johnson appointed Hamlin collector of the Port of Boston. He later resigned because of his disagreement with Johnson's policies on Reconstruction. Reelected to the Senate in 1869, Hamlin served until ill health caused his retirement in 1880. Retiring to Maine, Hamlin made his last public appearance at a Lincoln's birthday dinner in 1891.

VICE PRESIDENT

Andrew Johnson
(1808–1875)

CHRONOLOGICAL EVENTS

1808	Born, Raleigh, North Carolina, 29 December
1828	Elected alderman of Greeneville, Tennessee
1830	Elected mayor of Greeneville, Tennessee
1843	Elected to U.S. House of Representatives
1857	Elected to U.S. Senate
1862	Appointed military governor of Tennessee
1864	Elected vice president
1865	Became president upon the death of Abraham Lincoln
1875	Again elected to U.S. Senate
1875	Died, Carter Station, Tennessee, 31 July

BIOGRAPHY

A scrappy, self-made man, Andrew Johnson was born in a log cabin in North Carolina and apprenticed to a tailor as a boy. When he fled, his employer advertised a reward for his return. Johnson made his way to Greeneville, Tennessee, where he worked as a tailor and married Eliza McCardle. She helped him learn to read and educate himself. The industrious Johnson prospered as a tailor, invested in land, and owned several slaves. He became mayor of Greeneville and went to the Tennessee state legislature as a Jacksonian Democrat.

A forceful debater, he won election to the U.S. House of Representatives. Johnson always presented himself as a man of the common people. In Congress, he vigorously opposed the Whigs' legislative programs but also distanced himself from Southern aristocrats in his own party. Elected governor of Tennessee, he established a public education system in the state. In 1856, he was elected to the U.S. Senate. After Abraham Lincoln's election in 1860 caused the South to secede, Johnson called on Tennessee to remain in the Union. He was the only Southern senator not to resign when his state seceded.

Once the Union army captured much of Tennessee, President Lincoln appointed Johnson as the state's military governor. Although still a Democrat, Johnson denounced the state's wealthy planters and supported emancipation of their slaves. His stand won national acclaim from Republicans. In 1864, the Republican convention chose Johnson over the incumbent vice president, Hannibal Hamlin, to attract other War Democrats to a fusion ticket.

At his inauguration, Johnson suffered from typhoid fever and drank whiskey to fortify himself. Intoxicated, he delivered a rambling, incoherent inaugural address. Mortified Republicans in Congress called for his resignation, but President Lincoln defended him. Johnson was vice president for only six weeks when Lincoln was assassinated.

Thrust into the presidency, Johnson clashed repeatedly with Radical Republicans in Congress and vetoed their Reconstruction legislation. The Radicals' effort to remove him from office failed by a single vote in 1868. Johnson returned to Tennessee, where he later won another election to the U.S. Senate as a means of achieving personal satisfaction.

THE CABINET

SECRETARY OF STATE
William H. Seward, 1861, 1865

SECRETARY OF WAR
Joseph Holt, 1861
Simon Cameron, 1861
Edwin M. Stanton, 1862, 1865

SECRETARY OF THE TREASURY
John A. Dix, 1861
Salmon P. Chase, 1861
William P. Fessenden, 1864
Hugh McCulloch, 1865

POSTMASTER GENERAL
Horatio King, 1861
Montgomery Blair, 1861
William Dennison, 1864, 1865

ATTORNEY GENERAL
Edward Bates, 1861
James Speed, 1864, 1865

SECRETARY OF THE NAVY
Gideon Welles, 1861, 1865

SECRETARY OF THE INTERIOR
Caleb B. Smith, 1861
John P. Usher, 1863, 1865

(Courtesy Library of Congress.)

Montgomery Blair (1813–1883). Blair was appointed postmaster general by President Abraham Lincoln in 1861. He organized the army postal system and introduced free city mail delivery.

In 1864, Blair was forced to resign from the cabinet by the Radical Republicans because of his support for Lincoln's reconstruction plan for the South. In the 1868 election, he backed Democratic candidate Horatio Seymour and opposed the plans of the Radical Republicans for the reconstruction the South.

In 1876, Blair acted as Democratic candidate Samuel J. Tilden's counsel before the Electoral Commission, which investigated the disputed electoral votes in the election. The Commission, however, awarded the votes to Republican candidate Rutherford B. Hayes.

(Courtesy Library of Congress.)

Edwin M. Stanton (1814–1869). Stanton was appointed secretary of war by President Abraham Lincoln in 1862. He had previously served as attorney general in the administration of James Buchanan.

Stanton replaced Simon Cameron in the War Department. Cameron had recommended the arming of slaves. It was this proposal, offensive to Lincoln, which paved the way for Stanton's appointment.

As secretary of war, Stanton reorganized the department. He revoked war contracts tainted with fraud and prosecuted the perpetrators. Stanton promptly put himself in close contact with generals, governors, and others having to do with military affairs and especially with the congressional Committee on the Conduct of the War. Quick to make decisions and a master of detail were qualities which made him an outstanding administrator.

At the request of President Johnson, Stanton retained his post after Lincoln's death and directed the demobilization of the Union armies. His views on how to reconstruct the South brought him into serious conflict with Johnson. The President suspected that Stanton was conspiring with the rising opposition within the Republican Party to Johnson's lenient plans for Southerners who had supported the Confederate cause.

In February 1868, Stanton was dismissed by President Johnson. He refused to give up the office and claimed protection under the Tenure of Office Act (1867) which required the president to seek the approval of the U.S. Senate before removing an executive official from office.

On 24 February 1868, the U.S. House of Representatives voted to impeach Johnson for his defiance of the Act. Stanton resigned his post in May 1868. In 1869, President Ulysses S. Grant nominated him to the Supreme Court. Stanton died before confirmation hearings.

FAMILY

CHRONOLOGICAL EVENTS

13 December 1818	Mary Todd born	4 April 1853	Son, Thomas (Tad), born
4 November 1842	Mary Todd married Abraham Lincoln	1862	Son, Willie, died
		15 April 1865	Abraham Lincoln died
1 August 1843	Son, Robert Todd, born	1871	Son, Thomas, died
21 December 1850	Son, William (Willie) Wallace, born	16 July 1882	Mary Todd Lincoln died

Mary Todd Lincoln was 42 years old when her husband was elected president. She had mental problems which were worsened by the Civil War and the death of Willie and another son in infancy. Born in Kentucky, her brother and three half brothers fought for the Confederacy. She was accused of being a Southern sympathizer and even a spy.

After the assassination of her husband and the death of Tad, she was committed to a mental institution. She was later released, and she died in Springfield, Illinois.

This picture was taken a few days before the Inaugural Ball in Mathew Brady's studio. Brady was one of the most important of America's early photographers. (Courtesy Library of Congress).

Robert Todd Lincoln left Harvard Law School to join General Ulysses S. Grant's staff toward the end of the war. He was a successful corporation lawyer, and he served as secretary of war in the administrations of Presidents James A. Garfield and Chester A. Arthur. President Benjamin Harrison appointed him U.S. minister to Great Britain.

Robert ended his career as president of the Pullman Company. He died at the age of 82, the last of Lincoln's descendants to bear his name. ▶

(Courtesy Library of Congress.)

(Courtesy Library of Congress.)

◀ When Tad was born, his father said that he was like a little tadpole, giving him his nickname. Secretary of War Edwin Stanton gave Tad the uniform and sword of a Union lieutenant, when he was about 12 years old.

▲ *Mary Todd Lincoln and Willie are seated on the left; Robert Todd is standing and Tad is at his father's side. Willie became ill shortly after his 11th birthday, and he died in the White House on 1 February 1862.* (Courtesy Library of Congress.)

PLACES

ABRAHAM LINCOLN BIRTHPLACE NATIONAL HISTORIC SITE

2995 Lincoln Farm Road
Hodgenville, Kentucky 42748
Tel: (502) 358-3874

This is an artist's conception of the cabin in which Lincoln was born. A replica of the cabin is in the Memorial Building at the Abraham Lincoln Birthplace National Historic Site, Kentucky.
(Courtesy National Park Service.)

Located approximately 47 miles south of Louisville. Can be reached via Route 61. Open daily, 1 June through Labor Day, from 8 A.M. to 6:45 P.M.; the rest of the year from 8 A.M. to 4:45 P.M. Closed Christmas. No admission fee. Walking tours available. Advance arrangements required for guided tours. Picnic areas and hiking trails provided. Special services and facilities available for handicapped visitors; ask for information and assistance at the visitor center. Administered by the National Park Service, U.S. Department of the Interior.

In December 1808, Lincoln's father, Thomas, purchased the 348-acre Sinking Spring farm on Nolin Creek, a few miles south of Hodgen's Mill. The family moved into a one-room log cabin near the Sinking Spring, the water supply after which the farm was named. The cabin was approximately 18 feet by 16 feet, with a dirt floor, one window, a shingled roof, a small fireplace, and a chimney made of clay, straw, and hardwood. In February 1809, Lincoln was born there. Two-and-a-half years later, the Lincolns moved 10 miles east to a farm on Knob Creek.

In 1860, the remains of a log cabin, originally thought to be those of the birthplace cabin, were removed from the Lincoln farm and taken to another farm a little over a mile to the north. In 1895, the cabin was purchased by A. W. Dennett of New York and returned to the Lincoln farm. It was then dismantled and taken to various expositions around the country. About five years later, Robert Collier (the publisher of Collier's Weekly), Mark Twain, Samuel Gompers, and William Jennings Bryan formed the Lincoln Farm Association in order to preserve Lincoln's birthplace and to establish a separate memorial to him. The association purchased the farm in 1905 and the cabin in 1906. It also raised $350,000 to build the memorial. In 1909, the cornerstone to the memorial building was laid by President Theodore Roosevelt. Two years later, the marble and granite memorial building, designed by John Russell Pope, was dedicated by President William H. Taft.

THE ABRAHAM LINCOLN BOYHOOD NATIONAL MEMORIAL

P.O. Box 1816 • Lincoln City, Indiana 47552 • Tel: (812) 937-4541

Located on Indiana Highway 162, four miles south of Dale. Open daily from 8 A.M. to 5 P.M. year-round. Closed Thanksgiving, Christmas, and New Year's Day. Admission fee, with discounts available. Education groups, children under 16, and senior citizens admitted free. Administered by the National Park Service, U.S. Department of the Interior.

◀ *The Memorial Visitor Center of the Lincoln Boyhood National Memorial, completed in 1943, was designed by Indiana architect Richard E. Bishop. The exterior contains five sculptured panels by E.H. Daniels, marking significant periods in the life of Lincoln.* (Courtesy National Park Service; photographer: Richard Frear.)

A replica of the Lincoln Boyhood Home is part of the Lincoln Living Historical Farm. The cabin is surrounded by an orchard and a garden. A smokehouse, a carpentry shop, and a barn are located nearby. The site also contains the grave of Lincoln's mother and a visitor center. (Courtesy National Park Service, Lincoln Boyhood National Memorial.) ▶

In 1811, the Lincoln family moved to a farm on Knob Creek, where young Lincoln attended his first school. Five years later, threatened by a land suit, Lincoln's father, Thomas, decided to move to Indiana. In December 1816, the family packed up all their belongings and started for Anderson's Ferry at the Ohio River. The journey was difficult, and the acres leading to the land claim had to be cleared by hand. Lincoln's father, with the help of neighbors, erected a cabin, finishing it within several weeks. The cabin was renovated by Lincoln's stepmother, Sarah, in 1819 (his mother, Nancy, had died in October of the previous year). The roof was finished, a wooden floor was laid, the fireplace was replaced, and a door was built. In 1829, the Lincolns decided to move to Illinois, where young Lincoln would spend the next 30 years of his life.

LINCOLN HOME NATIONAL HISTORIC SITE

413 South Eighth Street • Springfield, Illinois 62701-1905 • Tel: (217) 492-4150

Located near Capitol Avenue in downtown Springfield. Can be reached via the business bypass through Springfield from Interstate 55. Open daily from 9 A.M. to 5 P.M. Closed Thanksgiving, Christmas, and New Year's Day. No admission fee. Tour tickets available on a first-come, first-served basis at the visitor center, 426 South Seventh Street. Groups may reserve tickets in advance. Administered by the National Park Service, U.S. Department of the Interior.

The Lincoln home in Springfield, Illinois is the only house that President Lincoln ever owned. (Courtesy National Park Service.)

In 1837, Lincoln came to Springfield, Illinois as a young lawyer. Five years later, he married Mary Todd, and he purchased the house and lot at the northeast corner of Eighth and Jackson Streets in 1844. Lincoln purchased the house for $1,500 from Reverend Charles Dresser, who had married them a year-and-a-half earlier. He and his family would spend the next 17 years there. In 1856, the house was renovated and expanded to accommodate Lincoln's growing family.

In 1861, when Lincoln and his family left for Washington, D.C., the house was rented to Lucian Tilton, the president of the Great Western Railroad. After Lincoln's assassination, the house continued to be owned and rented out by Lincoln's family. His eldest son, Robert Todd Lincoln, eventually became the sole owner and, in 1887, he donated it to the State of Illinois. In 1972, the home came under the administration of the National Park Service.

The site consists of four city blocks and preserves fourteen houses that date from the Lincoln era. A visitor center, which houses two theaters and historical exhibits, and a bookstore, operated by the Eastern National Park & Monument Association, are also located on the site.

LINCOLN'S TOMB STATE HISTORIC SITE

Oak Ridge Cemetery • Springfield, Illinois 62702 • Tel: (217) 782-2717

Located on the grounds of the Oak Ridge Cemetery in Springfield. Open daily, March through October, from 9 A.M. to 5 P.M.; November through February from 9 A.M. to 4 P.M. Closed Thanksgiving, Christmas, New Year's Day, and Martin Luther King, Jr., Presidents', Veterans', and General Election days. No admission fee. Groups of 25 or more must make advance reservations. Both the interior of the tomb and the restrooms are handicapped accessible. Managed by the Illinois Historic Preservation Agency.

The National Lincoln Monument Association was formed six days after Lincoln's assassination, and Governor Richard Oglesby was selected to preside over it. The new organization launched a nationwide drive for funds, collecting donations from schoolchildren, veterans' groups, church organizations, Sunday schools, and military units. The rest was supplemented by state funds.

The association selected Mather Square, the site of the present state capitol building, as the site for the monument. Mrs. Lincoln disliked the choice because she wanted her husband to be buried on consecrated ground. The association disregarded her wishes until she threatened to bring Lincoln's body back to Washington, D.C. In June 1865, the association agreed to build the monument at Oak Ridge Cemetery, and the city of Springfield donated six acres in the cemetery for its construction. A temporary tomb was then constructed to house the bodies of Lincoln and two of his sons, Edward and William.

In 1876 (11 years after Lincoln's death), a counterfeiting ring plotted to steal Lincoln's body. They were going to hold it for a $200,000 ransom plus the release of the counterfeiters' star engraver from Joliet State Prison. The attempt was unsuccessful, and—as a protective measure—Lincoln's body was temporarily hidden in the labyrinth of passageways beneath the obelisk. It was not until 1901 that Lincoln attained final rest. Under Robert Lincoln's instructions, a hole was dug 13 feet deep below the main catacomb floor. A four-foot base of cement was laid and an iron cage was sunk into it. At the final burial ceremony, the coffin was lowered into the cage and cement was poured, creating a block eight feet long by eight feet deep. The remains of President Lincoln, his wife and three of his four sons are interred in the tomb.

Construction began in 1869, and the 117-foot-tall granite tomb was dedicated five years later. In 1895, the National Lincoln Monument Association deeded the tomb and its surrounding grounds to the State of Illinois. (Courtesy Illinois Historic Preservation Agency.)

LINCOLN MEMORIAL

The National Mall at Twenty-third Street between Independence and Constitution Avenues, NW
Washington, D.C. • Tel: (202) 426-6841

> *Located at the west end of the Mall, near the Potomac River and Arlington Memorial Bridge. Open daily from 8 A.M. to midnight. Closed Christmas. No admission fee. Handicapped accessible. Special tours available. Visitor center and gift shop. Overlooks the Reflecting Pool and is opposite the Washington Monument. For more information, write: National Park Service, Mall Operations, 900 Ohio Drive, SW, Washington, D.C. 20242. A unit of the National Park System.*

Specifications:

Cornerstone Laid	*12 February 1915*
Dedicated	*30 May 1922*
Height	*80 feet (24 meters)*
Length	*189 feet (58 meters)*
Width	*118 2/3 feet (36.2 meters)*

In 1963, Dr. Martin Luther King, Jr., delivered his famous "I Have a Dream" speech from the steps of the memorial. (Courtesy Library of Congress.) ▶

In 1911, Congress passed a law creating the Lincoln Memorial Commission, which chose the site and the design by Henry Bacon. The memorial is a massive white marble building resembling a classic Greek temple. The Great Hall is surrounded by 36 columns representing the states of the Union at the time of Lincoln's assassination. The 48 states that existed at the time the memorial was dedicated are represented by the outside decorations. The interior is divided into three sections. The center section is dominated by the massive marble statue of Lincoln by Daniel Chester French. The two side sections contain tablets engraved with the Gettysburg Address and Lincoln's Second Inaugural Address, and two paintings: *Reunion* and *Emancipation*, both by Jules Guerin.

In 1922, Chief Justice William Howard Taft, chairman of the commission, presented the memorial to President Warren G. Harding, who accepted it on behalf of the United States.

▲ *The statue of Lincoln is by Daniel Chester French. It is 19 feet (5.8 meters) tall.* (Photograph by Maribeth A. Corona)

Andrew Johnson

17TH PRESIDENT
OF THE UNITED STATES OF AMERICA

CHRONOLOGICAL EVENTS

29 December 1808	Born, Raleigh, North Carolina
1822	Became apprenticed to tailor
1827	Moved to Greeneville, Tennessee
1828	Elected alderman, Greeneville, Tennessee
1830	Elected mayor, Greeneville, Tennessee
1835	Elected to Tennessee state legislature
1839	Reelected to Tennessee state legislature
1841	Elected to Tennessee State Senate
1843	Elected to U.S. House of Representatives
1853	Elected governor of Tennessee
1855	Reelected governor
1857	Elected to U.S. Senate
1860	Supported southern Democrat John C. Breckinridge for president
December 1860	Opposed secession of Southern states in U.S. Senate speech
4 March 1862	Appointed military governor of Tennessee
8 November 1864	Elected vice president
15 April 1865	Became president upon the death of Abraham Lincoln
19 February 1866	Vetoed Freedmen's Bureau Act
27 March 1866	Vetoed Civil Rights Act
2 March 1867	Vetoed Tenure of Office Act
2 March 1867	Vetoed First Reconstruction Act
23 March 1867	Vetoed Second Reconstruction Act
30 March 1867	Treaty for the purchase of Alaska signed
24 February 1868	Impeached by U.S. House of Representatives
16 May 1868	Acquitted by U.S. Senate
28 May 1868	Accepted resignation of Secretary of War Edwin M. Stanton
April 1869	Retired to Greeneville, Tennessee
January 1875	Again elected to U.S. Senate
31 July 1875	Died, Carter Station, Tennessee

BIOGRAPHY

Andrew Johnson was the first president of the United States to hold that office as a result of the assassination of his predecessor. He is the only president who never attended school for even a single day. He also is the only president to have been impeached by the U.S. House of Representatives. He remained in office because the U.S. Senate failed by one vote to convict him of the charges brought against him by the House.

EARLY YEARS. Andrew Johnson was born in a small, two-story house on 29 December 1808 in Raleigh, North Carolina. Neither his father nor his mother could read. His father, Jacob, was a bank porter as well as the city bell ringer. He drowned when Johnson was three years old. His mother, Mary McDonough Johnson, known as "Polly the Weaver," worked as a seamstress and laundress. When Johnson was 10 years old, his mother apprenticed him to a the tailor, to learn the trade. At age 15, Johnson, accompanied by his older brother, William, fled from their master, who posted a $10 reward for their return. Johnson walked 50 miles to Carthage, where he found employment as a journeyman tailor. Fearful of being arrested as long as he remained in North Carolina, he left after a few months. This time he crossed the state line into South Carolina, where he worked as a tailor. Eventually he settled in Greeneville, Tennessee, where he opened his own shop at age 18.

Johnson was a self-taught man who was eager for learning. He was 18 years old when he married Eliza McCardle, the daughter of a local shoemaker. She could read and write and helped her husband to improve his own skills. Although they were married for nearly 50 years and had five children, little is known about her. As First Lady, she rarely appeared in public, allowing her eldest daughter, Martha, to preside over social functions.

Johnson was fascinated by the speeches of great English statesmen and in time developed his own speaking skills. At age 21, he was elected a Greeneville alderman; his colleagues chose him to be mayor in 1830. In 1835, he was elected as a Democrat to the Tennessee state legislature, where he championed the rights of free laborers, small farmers, and tradesmen, whom he called "the plebeians." He opposed the political power of the slaveholders. He also spoke against nullification, a controversial policy that would have allowed states to ignore selected federal laws.

EARLY POLITICAL CAREER. Johnson continued his rise up the political ladder, winning election to the U.S. House of Representatives, where he served from 1843 to 1853. He voted in favor of the admission of Texas (1845), supported the war with Mexico (1848), and voted for the Compromise of 1850. He did vote to keep the "gag rule," a rule that prevented the House from considering anti-slavery petitions. In the reapportionment that occurred after the 1850 census, the boundaries of Johnson's congressional district were redrawn, and he lost many of his supporters. As a result, in 1852, Johnson chose to run for governor of Tennessee.

Johnson served two terms as governor of Tennessee (1853–1857). He supported a state public school system and favored the cultural development of the state, including the creation of a state library. When in Congress he had opposed many of the expenditures of the Smithsonian Institution and the construction of other federal buildings in the nation's capital, but in Tennessee he saw the need for such things.

In 1857, the Tennessee state legislature unanimously elected Johnson to the U.S. Senate, where he served until 1862. While in the Senate, Johnson defended slavery, supporting such measures as the Fugitive Slave Law, which allowed runaway slaves to be returned to their masters. But he remained strongly pro-Union, criticizing both those in favor of abolishing slavery and those who sought to preserve slavery by secession from the Union. He tried to keep Tennessee within the Union, but when his state seceded in 1861, he became the only senator from a seceding state to remain loyal to the Union and to keep his seat in the Senate. Many in Tennessee and throughout the Confederacy considered Johnson a traitor. But in the North, he became a hero for standing alone against secession.

President Abraham Lincoln appointed Johnson military governor of Tennessee in 1862. In this post, Johnson used his considerable wartime powers to rid the state of Confederate influences

Abraham Lincoln and Andrew Johnson easily defeated their Democratic contenders, George B. McClellan and George Pendleton. They received 55 percent of the popular vote and received 212 votes in the Electoral College. McClellan received 21 electoral votes.

This print shows Union heroes of the Civil War. Navy commanders, David Porter, David Faragut, and John Dahlgren, are on the left and army commanders, William T. Sherman, Ulysses S. Grant, and Philip Sheridan, are on the right.

George Washington is shown between Abraham Lincoln and Andrew Johnson. (Courtesy Collection of David J. and Janice L. Frent.)

and to support and assist Union troops within the state. Johnson convinced Lincoln to exempt Tennessee from the provisions of the Emancipation Proclamation on the grounds that preserving the Union was more important than ending slavery. As a reward for his loyalty to the Union, and in a symbolic attempt to balance his presidential ticket, Lincoln chose Johnson, a pro-Union Democrat from the South, to be his running mate in the presidential election of 1864. Lincoln won that election in both the popular vote and the electoral vote, with the 11 states of the Confederacy not participating. Johnson served as vice president for just over a month. Upon Lincoln's assassination, he became president on 15 April 1865.

PRESIDENCY AND IMPEACHMENT. Few men had come to the presidency with more overall experience as an elected official and an administrator at all levels of government than Andrew Johnson. But the extraordinary circumstances that placed him in the presidency made his tenure as president rough, stormy, and out of step with the political climate of that time. He set out to follow Lincoln's plan of charity and kindness toward the Confederate states, which held that the rebel states had never left the Union. This plan of constitutional Reconstruction required the rebel states to establish new state constitutions that abolished slavery and rejected secession. Citizenship could be restored with a simple oath of allegiance to the federal government. But this plan ran into serious opposition from the South, which was unwilling to share political power with newly enfranchised free African Americans. Furthermore, in the North, Radical Republicans, led by Thaddeus Stevens of Pennsylvania, the powerful leader in the House of Representatives, and Charles Sumner of Massachusetts in the U.S. Senate, wanted to punish the South by breaking the political stranglehold of the slaveholding class and preventing former slave owners from holding power. In the political struggle between Johnson and the Radical Republicans in Congress, the

President vetoed 29 bills, only to have Congress override 15 of his vetoes.

The tug-of-war between Congress and the President over the course of Reconstruction heated up after the congressional election of 1866, which found Northern voters in sympathy with the plans of the Radical Republicans. To keep Johnson from removing high government officials in sympathy with the Radicals, Congress passed the Tenure of Office Act in March 1867. Johnson vetoed the measure, declaring it an unconstitutional infringement on powers granted solely to the president. On 12 August 1867, Johnson, in defiance of this act, suspended Secretary of War Edwin M. Stanton while the Senate was not in session. When the Senate returned Johnson notified it of his decision to suspend the secretary and the Senate refused to agree with his action. Then, on 21 February 1868, Johnson removed Stanton from office. Three days later, the House of Representatives began impeachment proceedings against the President for "high crimes and misdemeanors" because of his violation of the Tenure of Office Act. While the articles of impeachment contained 11 separate charges against the President, 9 of them related to the single act of firing Stanton. The remaining two articles listed a series of instances when the President had "in a loud voice" spoken out against the actions of Congress related to the Reconstruction policy, accusing the Thirty-ninth Congress, in one instance, of failing to represent all the states.

The House of Representatives approved the articles of impeachment and presented them to the Senate on 4 March 1868. Under the U.S. Constitution, the House brings the charges of impeachment, and the Senate, with the Chief Justice of the United States presiding, tries the case. A two-thirds vote of the Senate is required for conviction. Beginning on 16 May 1868 and concluding on 26 May 1868, with an adjournment for the Republican National Convention, the Senate voted separately on three of the articles, and in each case it failed by one vote to get the

THIRD ANNUAL MESSAGE

. . . It will hardly be necessary to call the attention of Congress to the subject of providing for the payment to Russia of the sum stipulated in the treaty for the cession of Alaska. Possession having been formally delivered to our commissioner, the territory remains for the present in care of a military force, awaiting such civil organization as shall be directed by Congress. . . .

• *William E. Seward, secretary of state under President Andrew Johnson, wanted the United States to annex Canada, Hawaii, and several Caribbean islands. Although he did not achieve this goal, Seward was successful in purchasing Alaska from Russia in 1867 for $7.2 million—less than two cents an acre. Twice the size of Texas, this vast area was inhabited by less than 20,000 people, mainly Eskimos.*

In his Third Annual Message (3 December 1867), President Johnson requested that Congress allocate funds to pay for Alaska.

President Andrew Johnson, General Ulysses S. Grant, and Secretary of War Edwin M. Stanton reviewed General William T. Sherman's army on 24 May 1865. Less than three years later, President Johnson fired Stanton, who was undermining his policies. This led to Johnson's impeachment. (The Soldier in Our Civil War, Courtesy Collection of Charles E. Smith.)

VETO OF FIRST RECONSTRUCTION ACT

I have examined the bill "to provide for the more efficient government of the rebel States" with the care and anxiety which its transcendent importance is calculated to awaken. I am unable to give it my assent, for reasons so grave that I hope a statement of them may have some influence on the minds of the patriotic and enlightened men with whom the decision must ultimately rest.

I submit to Congress whether this measure is not in its whole character, scope, and object without precedent and without authority, in palpable conflict with the plainest provisions of the Constitution, and utterly destructive to those great principles of liberty and humanity for which our ancestors on both sides of the Atlantic have shed so much blood and expended so much treasure.

The ten States named in the bill are divided into five districts. For each district an officer of the Army, not below the rank of brigadier-general, is to be appointed to rule over the people; and he is to be supported with an efficient military force to enable him to perform his duties and enforce his authority. Those duties and that authority, as defined by the third section of the bill, are "to protect all persons in their rights of person and property, to suppress insurrection, disorder, and violence, and to punish or cause to be punished all disturbers of the public peace or criminals." The power thus given to the commanding officer over all the people of each district is that of an absolute monarch. His mere will is to take the place of all law. . . .

It is plain that the authority here given to the military officer amounts to absolute despotism. But to make it still more unendurable, the bill provides that it may be delegated to as many subordinates as he chooses to appoint, for it declares that he shall "punish or cause to be punished." Such a power has not been wielded by any monarch in England for more than five hundred years. In all that time no people who speak the English language have borne such servitude. It reduces the whole population of the ten States—all persons, of every color, sex, and condition, and every stranger within their limits—to the most abject and degrading slavery. No master ever had a control so absolute over the slaves as this bill gives to the military officers over both white and colored persons. . . .

The United States are bound to guarantee to each State a republican form of government. Can it be pretended that this obligation is not palpably broken if we carry out a measure like this, which wipes away every vestige of republican government in ten States and puts the life, property, liberty, and honor of all the people in each of them under the domination of a single person clothed with unlimited authority? . . .

The bill also denies the legality of the governments of ten of the States which participated in the ratification of the amendment to the Federal Constitution abolishing slavery forever within the jurisdiction of the United States and practically excludes them from the Union. If this assumption of the bill be correct, their concurrence cannot be considered as having been legally given, and the important fact is made to appear that the consent of three-fourths of the States—the requisite number—has not been constitutionally obtained to the ratification of that amendment, thus leaving the question of slavery where it stood before the amendment was officially declared to have become a part of the Constitution. . . .

• *President Johnson vetoed this Act on 2 March 1867, and Congress overrode his veto on the same day. Southern states were required to call new state constitutional conventions elected by universal manhood suffrage. The Act mandated that each state had to guarantee African American males the right to vote and that each state had to ratify the Fourteenth Amendment. Former Confederates were excluded from voting. Congress would end military rule when it felt the Act had achieved its goal.*

The Impeachment Committee of the U.S. House of Representatives consisted of seven members of Congress. The Chairman was Thaddeus Stevens of Pennsylvania. They presented the 11 articles of impeachment to the U.S. Senate on 4 March 1868. The House had already voted to impeach President Johnson by a vote of 126 to 47 on 24 February 1868.

Front row, left to right, Benjamin Butler of Massachusetts; Thaddeus Stevens of Pennsylvania; Thomas Williams of Pennsylvania; and John A. Bingham of Ohio. Back row, left to right, James F. Wilson of Iowa; George Sewall Boutwell of Massachusetts; and John A. Logan of Illinois. (Courtesy National Archives.)

two-thirds majority required. Seven Republican senators joined with the Democrats to block the conviction. The remaining articles were never brought to a vote. The President was thus acquitted of all charges. He had been impeached by the House, but since the Senate did not convict him he remained in office until the end of his term.

Johnson presided over a nation still divided as a result of the Civil War and also divided over the best way politically to reconstruct the former rebel states. He ascended to the presidency following the tragic assassination of Abraham Lincoln, the first such case in the history of the nation. He was a southern Democrat, even though he had been Lincoln's running mate. He tried to lead a government dominated by northern

ARTICLE ONE OF IMPEACHMENT

ARTICLE I. That said Andrew Johnson, President of the United States, on the 21st day of February, A.D. 1868, at Washington, in the District of Columbia, unmindful of the high duties of his office, of his oath of office, and of the requirement of the Constitution that he should take care that the laws be faithfully executed, did unlawfully and in violation of the Constitution and laws of the United States issue an order in writing for the removal of Edwin M. Stanton from the office of Secretary for the Department of War, said Edwin M. Stanton having been theretofore duly appointed and commissioned, by and with the advice and consent of the Senate of the United States, as such Secretary; and said Andrew Johnson, President of the United States, on the 12th day of August, A.D. 1867, and during the recess of said Senate, having suspended by his order Edwin M. Stanton from said office, and within twenty days after the first day of the next meeting of said Senate—that is to say, on the 12th day of December, in the year last aforesaid—having reported to said Senate such suspension, with the evidence and reasons for his action in the case and the name of the person designated to perform the duties of such office temporarily until the next meeting of the Senate; and said Senate thereafterwards, on the 13th day of January, A.D. 1868, having duly considered the evidence and reasons reported by said Andrew Johnson for said suspension, and having refused to concur in said suspension, whereby and by force of the provisions of an act entitled "An act regulating the tenure of certain civil offices," passed March 2, 1867, said Edwin M. Stanton did forthwith resume the functions of his office, whereof the said Andrew Johnson had then and there due notice; and said Edwin M. Stanton, by reason of the premises, on said 21st day of February, being lawfully entitled to hold said office of Secretary for the Department of War; which said order for the removal of said Edwin M. Stanton is in substance as follows; that is to say:

EXECUTIVE MANSION,
Washington, D.C., February 21, 1868.

HON. EDWIN M. STANTON,
        Washington, D.C.

SIR: By virtue of the power and authority vested in me as President by the Constitution and laws of the United States, you are hereby removed from office as Secretary for the Department of War, and your functions as such will terminate upon the receipt of this communication.

You will transfer to Brevet Major-General Lorenzo Thomas, Adjutant-General of the Army, who has this day been authorized and empowered to act as Secretary of War ad interim, all records, books, papers, and other public property now in your custody and charge.

Respectfully, yours,

ANDREW JOHNSON.

• *The Tenure of Office Act (1867) prohibited the president from removing officials appointed by and with the advice of the Senate without the approval of the Senate. Nine of the articles of Impeachment brought against President Johnson related to his dismissal of Secretary of War Edwin M. Stanton and the consequent violation of the Act.*

THE SENATE VOTE ON ARTICLE ELEVEN OF IMPEACHMENT
THE UNITED STATES v. ANDREW JOHNSON, PRESIDENT

The Chief Justice of the Supreme Court stated that, in pursuance of the order of the Senate, he would first proceed to take the judgment of the Senate on the eleventh article. The roll of the Senate was called, with the following result:

The Senators who voted "guilty" were Messrs. Anthony, Cameron, Cattell, Chandler, Cole, Conkling, Conness, Corbett, Cragin, Drake, Edmunds, Ferry, Frelinghuysen, Harlan, Howard, Howe, Morgan, Morrill of Maine, Morrill of Vermont, Morton, Nye, Patterson of New Hampshire, Pomeroy, Ramsey, Sherman, Sprague, Stewart, Summer, Thayer, Tipton, Wade, Williams, Willey, Wilson, and Yates—35.

The Senators who voted "not guilty" were Messrs. Bayard, Buckalew, Davis, Dixon, Doolittle, Fessenden, Fowler, Grimes, Henderson, Hendricks, Johnson, McCreery, Norton, Patterson of Tennessee, Ross, Saulsbury, Trumbull, Van Winkle, and Vickers—19.

The Chief Justice announced that upon this article thirty-five Senators had voted "guilty" and nineteen Senators "not guilty," and declared that two-thirds of the Senators present not having pronounced him guilty, Andrew Johnson, President of the United States, stood acquitted of the charges contained in the eleventh article of impeachment.

• On 16 May 1868, the U.S. Senate voted on Article Eleven of the impeachment proceedings. It referred to President Johnson's violation of the Tenure of Office Act. The Senate then went into recess so that the Republicans could attend their national convention in Chicago.

This ticket admitted the bearer to the impeachment trial of President Johnson. (Courtesy Collection of David J. and Janice L. Frent.)

Mathew Brady took this picture of Andrew Johnson in his Washington gallery shortly before Johnson's inauguration as president.

"Johnson sought political power throughout his entire adult life. Ironically for him, and tragically for the nation, when he acquired, as a result of an assassin's bullet, the power of the presidency, he proved incapable of using it in a positive and effective fashion. Although he possessed great courage and determination, sincere and strong convictions, and considerable natural ability, he lacked most of the other qualities of a true statesman, notably tact, flexibility, and insight and foresight. Consequently he failed greatly in meeting the great challenges that faced him in dealing with Reconstruction. He was the wrong man in the wrong place at the wrong time." Albert Castel, *"Johnson, Andrew,"* in Encyclopedia of the American Presidency, *edited by Leonard W. Levy and Louis Fisher.* (Courtesy National Archives.)

PROCLAMATION OF AMNESTY

. . . Whereas the authority of the Federal Government having been reestablished in all the States and Territories within the jurisdicition of the United States . . . that an universal amnesty and pardon for paritcipation in said rebellion extended to all who have borne any part therein will tend to secure permanient peace, order, and prosperity throughout the land, and to renew and fully restore confidence and fraternal feeling among the whole people, and their respect for and attachment to the National Government, designed by its patriotic founders for the general good:

Now, therefore, be it known that I, Andrew Johnson, President of the United States, by virtue of the power and authority in me vested by the Constitution and in the name of the sovereign people of the United States, do hereby proclaim and declare, unconditionally and without reservation, to all and to every person who, directly or indirectly, participated in the late insurrection or rebellion a full pardon and amnesty for the offense of treason against the United States or of adhering to their enemies during the late civil war, with restoration of all rights, privileges, and immunities under the Constitution and the laws which have been made in pursuance thereof.

• *On Christmas Day 1868, President Andrew Johnson, using authority granted to him by the Constitution, proclaimed a final and absolute amnesty "to all and to every person who, directly or indirectly, participated in the late insurrection or rebellion . . . with restoration of all rights, privileges, and immunities."*

Republicans in Congress and within his own administration. At the Republican convention of 1868, unpopular and wounded by the impeachment proceedings against him, he was not renominated for president. The nomination went instead to Ulysses S. Grant. Johnson's attempt to be lenient toward the South had failed in the surge of support for the sterner program of the Radical Republicans. During the war, Johnson had been accused of being a traitor in his own state of Tennessee, but when he returned to his home state in retirement, he was greeted with much ceremony as a "patriot." Johnson remained active in Democratic Party politics, campaigning on behalf of several Democratic candidates for Congress. He ran for the U.S. Senate in 1871 and for the U S. House of Representatives in 1872, failing in both instances. In the presidential election of 1872, he supported Horace Greeley, rather than his political enemy Ulysses S. Grant. Johnson's health was seriously weakened during a cholera epidemic in 1873. In 1875 the Tennessee state legislature elected him to the U.S. Senate, where he served for a few months before his death on 31 July 1875. He is the only president of the United States to serve in the Senate following his presidency.

THE CABINET

SECRETARY OF STATE
William H. Seward, 1865

SECRETARY OF WAR
Edwin M. Stanton, 1865, 1868
Ulysses S. Grant, 1867 [1]
John M. Schofield, 1868

SECRETARY OF THE TREASURY
Hugh McCulloch, 1865

POSTMASTER GENERAL
William Dennison, 1865
Alexander W. Randall, 1866

ATTORNEY GENERAL
James Speed, 1865
Henry Stanbery, 1866
William M. Everts, 1868

SECRETARY OF THE NAVY
Gideon Welles, 1865

SECRETARY OF THE INTERIOR
John P. Usher, 1865
James Harlan, 1865
Orville H. Browning, 1866

---

1. President Johnson appointed Grant secretary of war *ad interim*. He served 12 August 1867 to 14 January 1868.

(Courtesy Collection of Charles E. Smith.)

William H. Seward (1801–1872). Seward was appointed secretary of state by President Abraham Lincoln in 1861. Coinciding with Lincoln's assassination, he was wounded by a co-conspirator. He remained secretary of state when Andrew Johnson became president.

As secretary of state, Seward advocated a strong foreign policy. His most notable achievement was his successful negotiations with Great Britain over the *Trent* affair. (A U.S. ship captain had stopped the British steamer *Trent* and forcibly removed two Confederate commissioners and their secretaries. News of this provoked war fever in Great Britain.) Seward also defended President Johnson against the Radical Republicans during the impeachment trial.

In 1867, Seward, an expansionist, negotiated the purchase of Alaska from Russia for $7.2 million. This purchase was called "Seward's Folly" by those who did not see Alaska's potential.

FAMILY

CHRONOLOGICAL EVENTS

4 October 1810	Eliza McCardle born	22 February 1834	Son, Robert, born
17 May 1827	Eliza McCardle married Andrew Johnson	5 August 1852	Son, Andrew, Jr., born
		1863	Son, Charles, died
25 October 1828	Daughter, Martha, born	1869	Son, Robert, died
19 February 1830	Son, Charles, born	31 July 1875	Andrew Johnson died
8 May 1832	Daughter, Mary, born	15 January 1876	Eliza Johnson died

(Courtesy of Library of Congress.)

Eliza McCardle was 16 years old when she married Andrew Johnson. He was only two years older. While he worked in his tailor shop, she read to him and helped him to improve his very basic reading, spelling, and math skills.

The Johnsons had five children: Martha, Charles, Mary, Robert, and Andrew, Jr. Charles joined the Union army and died during the war, when he was thrown from his horse. Mary married Dan Stover, an officer in the Union army. After Stover's death in 1864, she brought her three children to live in the White House.

Robert was an officer in the Union army. He was also secretary to his father when he was president. He died at 35, an alcoholic. Andrew, Jr. founded a newspaper which failed after two years, and he died soon after that, at the age of 27.

Eliza Johnson was confined to a wheelchair by the time she joined her husband in the White House. She spent most of her time with her grandchildren and made only two public appearances.

Martha Johnson married Judge David T. Patterson. After the Civil War, he was a U.S. senator from Tennessee. Because of her mother's illness, she handled all the social responsibilities at the White House.

ANDREW JOHNSON NATIONAL HISTORIC SITE

Depot and College Streets • Greeneville, Tennessee 37743 • Tel: (615) 638-3551

Located approximately 30 miles southwest of Johnson City. Can be reached via U.S. 321 or U.S. 11E; the visitor center is located on Main Street. The site contains Johnson's two Greeneville residences (the early home of Johnson and the homestead), a visitor center, and the National Cemetery with gravesite and monument. The park units are open daily from 9 A.M. to 5 P.M. Closed Christmas. Admission fee. The visitor center, the early home of Johnson, and the cemetery are wheelchair accessible; the homestead is accessible on the first floor and basement level. Maintained and operated by the National Park Service, U.S. Department of the Interior.

During the Civil War, Johnson's home was occupied by Confederate troops and used as a hospital. It was also occupied by federal troops as late as 1868. (Courtesy Andrew Johnson National Historic Site.)

Johnson purchased the homestead in September 1851. The original home consisted of eight rooms on three levels. A second level and a rear porch were added between 1869 and 1870. Johnson lived there until his death in 1875. Ten years later, his daughter, Martha, remodeled the home into a Victorian-style house. The homestead continued to be remodeled and enlarged to its present size. Ten rooms, furnished with original family possessions, are open to the public.

◀ *Johnson's tailor shop became the center of village politics between 1831 and 1843. During this period, his forming of close political friendships with people in the working class greatly influenced his political career. The tailor shop is located inside the visitor center.* (Courtesy Andrew Johnson National Historic Site.)

The Johnson National Cemetery is located less than half a mile from the homestead. The Italian marble monument was dedicated in June 1878 by his surviving children; it stands 27 feet tall and is decorated with stars and stripes. An American eagle is perched on a globe directly above a scroll of the Constitution and an open Bible. The memorial inscription over his grave reads, "His Faith In The People Never Wavered." (Courtesy Library of Congress.) ▶

PRESIDENT ANDREW JOHNSON BIRTHPLACE

Mordecai Historic Park • One Mimosa Street • Raleigh, North Carolina 27604 • Tel: (919) 834-4844

Located on Village Street in Mordecai Historic Park. Open Monday through Friday from 10 A.M. to 3 P.M.; Saturday and Sunday from 1:30 P.M. to 3:30 P.M. Closed holidays. Admission fee, with discounts available for students and senior citizens. Children ages 6 and under admitted free. One-hour tours begin every half hour. Group tours by reservation. Maintained and operated by Capital Area Preservation, Inc., a nonprofit historic preservation organization, in cooperation with the Raleigh Department of Parks and Recreation.

Andrew Johnson was born on 29 December 1808 in a small, two-story house on Fayetteville Street in downtown Raleigh, North Carolina. The house, built around 1795, served as a kitchen for Casso's Inn, which was located across the street from the State House. Johnson's parents, Jacob and Mary, lived in the upstairs room where he was born. In 1812, Andrew's father died, and his mother then raised him and his brother, William. In 1826, Johnson moved to Greeneville, Tennessee, with his mother, stepfather Turner Dougherty, and brother.

The birthplace has been restored to its probable appearance at the time of Johnson's birth. The present furnishings were not owned by the Johnson family, but are authentic items of that period. The original structure was first moved to East Carrabus Street and then to Pullen Park, where it was purchased by the Wake County Committee of the Colonial Dames of America. The committee presented it to the City of Raleigh. In 1975, it was moved to its present location in Mordecai Historic Park.

Ulysses S. Grant

18TH PRESIDENT
OF THE UNITED STATES OF AMERICA

CHRONOLOGICAL EVENTS

27 April 1822	Born, Point Pleasant, Ohio
1 July 1843	Graduated from U.S. Military Academy, West Point, New York
1846–1848	Served in the Mexican War
September 1847	Promoted to first lieutenant
August 1853	Commissioned captain; assigned to Fort Humboldt, California
11 April 1854	Resigned commission in the army
May 1860	Worked in family's leather goods store in Galena, Illinois
17 June 1861	Appointed colonel of Twenty-first Illinois Infantry
7 August 1861	Appointed brigadier general of volunteers
February 1862	Captured Forts Henry and Donelson, Tennessee
6–7 April 1862	Battle of Shiloh, Tennessee
4 July 1863	Accepted surrender of Vicksburg, Mississippi
23–25 November 1863	Battle of Chattanooga, Tennessee
12 March 1864	Appointed general in chief of Union armies
9 April 1865	Accepted surrender of General Robert E. Lee at Appomattox Court House, Virginia
12 August 1867	Appointed secretary of war, *ad interim*
3 November 1868	Elected president
4 March 1869	Inaugurated president
30 March 1870	Fifteenth Amendment to Constitution ratified
8 May 1871	Treaty of Washington signed
5 November 1872	Reelected president
4 March 1873	Inaugurated president
1875	Whiskey Ring exposed
1880	Lost bid for presidential nomination
1884	Bankrupt due to faulty investments
June 1884	Wrote about Civil War experiences for *Century Magazine*
19 July 1885	Completed *Personal Memoirs of U.S. Grant*
23 July 1885	Died, Mount McGregor, New York

BIOGRAPHY

EARLY YEARS AND WEST POINT. Hiram Ulysses Grant was born in Point Pleasant, Ohio on 27 April 1822. His family moved to Georgetown, Ohio, where Grant, the eldest of three brothers and three sisters, lived until he was 17. Grant's father ran a tannery, a business that involved the slaughtering and skinning of animals and the curing of their skins in smelly chemical solutions. The tannery was a place that Grant always wanted to avoid, and his father permitted him to do other jobs. Grant developed a love for horses and was skillful at training and riding them.

Knowing that Grant had no interest in the tannery, his father arranged for his admission to the U.S. Military Academy at West Point in 1839. Arriving at the academy, he found himself registered in error under the name U.S. Grant. This was apparently the result of a mistake by the congressman who had submitted his nomination for entrance. Nonetheless, it was the name he used for the rest of his life.

Grant did fairly well at West Point but showed no great interest in a military career. Because of his love of horses, he tried upon graduation (at age 21) to get appointed to the cavalry but was assigned to the infantry. His first assignment was near St. Louis, Missouri, where he met Julia Dent, the sister of a West Point roommate. They married on 22 August 1848. Their union was a loving and lasting one that sustained him through many difficulties.

THE WAR WITH MEXICO. In 1845, Grant was sent to Texas as part of a force commanded by General Zachary Taylor. Grant later wrote in his personal memoirs that he felt that the United States had provoked the war with Mexico and that it was an unjust conflict fought in order to acquire territory.

Grant served as a quartermaster in the infantry, making him responsible for supplying and moving provisions and troops. He also participated in the fighting. This firsthand experience of the horrors of war left him feeling energized. He observed the styles of the various commanders, identifying with the quiet determination of General Taylor rather than the flashier style of General Winfield Scott.

BETWEEN WARS. In 1852, Grant was transferred to Fort Vancouver on the Pacific coast. There he attempted potato farming outside his regular army duties in order to raise money to bring his family to the West Coast. This was the first of many private

business failures that Grant had in his lifetime. Transferred to the San Francisco area under the command of an officer he disliked and suffering from a lack of money and from the absence of his family, Grant became depressed and began to drink. This led to the beginning of rumors which would follow him the rest of his life, that he was a drunk. In 1854, he resigned from the military and found himself at the age of 32, without a profession.

Grant joined his family in St. Louis. He began to farm land owned by his wife's brother. In 1856 his father-in-law gave him some land of his own. Grant was not successful, and in the winter he hauled firewood into St. Louis to sell on the street in order to raise money. By Christmas 1857, Grant had to pawn his watch to raise money. A fourth and last child was born in 1858, the year Grant gave up farming and began an unsuccessful attempt at operating a bill-collecting business.

When the Civil War began in 1861, Grant was nearing 40. He had resigned from the army and failed at farming and other business enterprises. He had been reduced to clerking in his father's store in Galena, Illinois, reporting to his younger brother, who ran the business. The Civil War, however, would change everything for Grant and for the nation.

THE CIVIL WAR YEARS. Until this point, Grant had not been actively involved in politics. His wife and her family in Missouri owned slaves, and Grant himself had owned one slave with whom he worked while farming, but he had given the man his freedom in 1859.

When South Carolina seceded from the United States in December 1860, Grant believed that the Union must be preserved. He felt that slavery would end once the South's economic dependence on cotton had been reduced by worldwide competition. Grant participated in the raising of volunteer Union troops in Galena. However, he refused any formal role with the volunteers, since he wanted to be reinstated in the regular army at the rank of colonel. After unsuccessful attempts to rejoin the regular army, he accepted appointment as a colonel in the Illinois volunteers. Grant did an excellent job preparing the troops during maneuvers in Missouri. In the summer of 1861, he, along with several other officers, was promoted to brigadier general.

Grant led Union troops in several battles in areas key to control of the Mississippi River. His capture of Fort Donelson in Tennessee (1862) was one of the first major Union victories of the Civil War. Despite his friendship, made during the Mexican War, with the opposing Confederate officer, Grant insisted on an unconditional surrender rather than accepting a more gentlemanly negotiated armistice in this battle. This decision set the tone for his determined prosecution of the war. It was the victory at Fort Donelson that brought Grant to President Abraham Lincoln's attention.

Grant fought a series of battles that were considered victories for the Union army, but at the cost of large losses of life on both sides. Grant understood that ultimate victory depended on a war in which the larger population and resources of the North would prevail. He fought that type of war and gained control of the Mississippi River. These battles brought Grant national publicity and confronted him with a new problem—what to do with the African Americans who fled from slavery during the victories over the Southern armies.

The escaped slaves were referred to as "contrabands." With no nationally defined policy to guide him, Grant determined that they had to be protected from Southern troops who might seek revenge. When the Emancipation Proclamation was issued on 1 January 1863, the slaves in the rebel states became freedmen, and tens of thousands of African Americans joined the Union army.

In October 1863, Grant was given command of Union troops in the West, and he moved to save the besieged garrison at Chattanooga, Tennessee. In recognition of Grant's achievement, President Lincoln had the rank of lieutenant general reestablished and he bestowed it on Grant. The rank had not been held by anyone since George Washington. In March 1864, Grant moved his family to Washington, D.C. and established his headquarters as commander of the army in Virginia.

Grant's popularity was enhanced by his quiet public manner. He indicated no desire for public office and therefore presented no political challenge to President Lincoln's 1864 renomination. During 1864, Grant directed the war and secured victories that guaranteed Lincoln's reelection, including General William Tecumseh Sherman's taking of Atlanta, Georgia in September 1864. In December 1864, Nashville, Tennessee fell and Sherman finished his famed "March to the Sea," ending in the capture of Savannah, Georgia. Grant kept pressure on the Confederate capital at Richmond, Virginia and was involved in many of the peace discussions that began even as the fighting continued. On 9 April 1865, the fully and freshly uniformed gentleman, General Robert E. Lee, surrendered his army at Appomattox Court House, Virginia. General Grant, an ordinary man to the end, wore a worn and dusty field uniform as he received Lee's surrender.

Lincoln and his cabinet, with Grant participating as head of the Union army, discussed how the United States was to be reunited or reconstructed, giving the name "Reconstruction" to the postwar period. Grant met with the cabinet and Lincoln on 14 April 1865 and was invited to attend the theater with Lincoln that evening. He declined, largely due to his wife's dislike of Mrs. Lincoln. Lincoln was assassinated that evening in what is believed to have been a conspiracy by angry Southerners that was aimed as well at others in the cabinet and at Grant. Vice President Andrew Johnson became president.

THE RECONSTRUCTION ERA. President Johnson assigned Grant in the fall of 1865 to tour the South and to report on Reconstruction. He reported favorably on the idea of returning control of the South to fair-minded Southerners. He felt that they would come to a reasonable accommodation with the freed slaves, particularly if the former slaves were supported by the Freedmen's Bureau. The Bureau had been created in March 1865 to help the freed slaves to become integrated, both economically and educationally, into Southern society.

Grant was caught between the desire of President Johnson simply to turn over to those who had previously controlled it and the demands of the Radical Republicans in Congress who wanted to ensure equal rights and opportunities for the African Americans in the South. He tried to stay neutral. Violence broke out against African Americans and their white supporters in various places in the former slave states. The U.S. Army under Grant took action in some places, since it was the only body capable of putting down or preventing violence that often was instigated or ignored by the local police authorities.

The clash between Congress and President Johnson over Reconstruction grew worse. Johnson dismissed Secretary of War Edward M. Stanton and named General Grant to the position on a temporary basis. Johnson was trying to avoid having to seek U.S. Senate approval for the appointment. When the Senate reappointed Stanton in January 1868 over

▲ *Mathew Brady took this picture of Grant at City Point, Virginia after he was promoted to lieutenant general. Soon after this picture was taken, Grant's army fought the Battle of Spotsylvania on 10 May 1864.* (Courtesy Library of Congress.)

▲ *H. A. Ogden, the famous nineteenth-century military artist, called this painting "Grant in the Wilderness, May 5 1864."* (Courtesy Collection of Charles E. Smith.)

Grant took the Army of the Potomac, nearly 120,000 men, across the Rapidan River in northern Virginia on 3 May 1864 to encounter Robert E. Lee and his army of some 65,000. Four days of fighting resulted in approximately 28,000 casualties.

Of this campaign, historian William S. McFeely wrote: "In May 1864 Ulysses Grant began a vast campaign that was a hideous disaster in every respect but one — it worked. He led his troops into the Wilderness and there produced a nightmare of inhumanity and inept military strategy that ranks with the worst such episodes in the history of warfare."

• *William S. McFeely,* Grant: A Biography.

Johnson's objections, Grant gave up the post, angering Johnson. The fighting between Congress and President Johnson led to Johnson's impeachment by the House and his trial before the Senate, which failed to convict him in May 1868. The public did not blame Grant for the conflict, and he emerged as the popular candidate in the 1868 presidential race.

THE PRESIDENCY. Grant was nominated for the presidency by the Republican convention while remaining in Washington as head of the army. His written acceptance speech included what became a campaign slogan: "Let us have peace." Without being specific, the slogan seemed to refer to the conflict between Johnson and Congress, the continuing violence in the South against African Americans during Reconstruction, the remaining anger left over from the Civil War, and the nation's combative policy toward Native Americans in the West. Grant moved back to Galena, Illinois, while others campaigned on his behalf. He did travel as part of his army command to view the Indian war territories in the West. On his return through Chicago, thousands of tanners turned out to salute him and to confirm his public image as an ordinary citizen.

Grant and his vice presidential running mate, Schuyler Colfax, won the election. They defeated Horatio Seymour and Frank Blair, receiving a popular vote of 52.7 percent. They received 214 votes in the Electoral College compared to 80 votes for the Democrats. In his inaugural speech on 4 March 1869, Grant indicated his intention to support Reconstruction as Congress wished. He also stated his support for a strong currency backed by gold, and his desire for fairness for Native Americans, whom he referred to as the "original occupants of this land."

Grant appointed a cabinet split between Radical Republican supporters of Reconstruction and others whose support for African Americans was weak. The cabinet membership shifted constantly. By 1870 Attorney General Amos Akerman took a firm role in enforcing federal laws passed to protect African Americans' rights in the South. Federal forces intervened in some states to limit the power of the Ku Klux Klan, which had started its terrorist operations in 1866. Grant, however, was often inconsistent or late in his use of federal power, and African Americans and their white supporters in

the South were often intimidated by white supremacists. Grant was firmer in his support for the Fifteenth Amendment, which was ratified in 1870 and which provided voting rights to male African Americans. Despite these federal efforts, Grant's attempts to ensure fairness for African Americans in the South failed as Southern states reentered the Union and old-line conservatives took over the governments in those states.

Grant's policy toward Native Americans combined a desire to convert the tribes to Christianity and a wish to have honest missionaries replace the often corrupt Indian agents who provided supplies to Native Americans. Grant's peace policy placed the Native Americans on reservations with the ultimate goal of assimilating them into American culture, rather than preserving their own culture. It was, however, a humane policy compared to the policies of those who sought to kill all Native Americans who fought the nation's westward expansion.

Grant's administration suffered from repeated problems of internal corruption. One of the first claims of corruption arose in September 1869 when financiers manipulated gold prices on "Black Friday" on the basis of information obtained through one of Grant's relatives. Although Grant himself was not involved, a congressional investigation heard unproved rumors that Grant's wife had a financial interest in the manipulation. Another scandal surfaced when Grant attempted to annex the Dominican Republic for possible use as a homeland for African Americans facing persecution in the South. The annexation was rejected in 1871 by senators who preferred to seek equality within the United States for African Americans. Some senators had heard charges that Grant's personal White House aide, Orville Babcock, would benefit from the annexation because he owned land in the Dominican Republic. These and other charges of corruption in government service led to attempts to reform civil service and to introduce merit examinations for government positions. Although a commission was formed to explore these issues, little real progress on eliminating political patronage was made during Grant's administration.

Grant was more successful in negotiations with Great Britain over boundary and fishing rights disputes and claims stemming from damages caused by Great Britain's building of five ships for the Confederacy during the Civil War. Named the "Alabama Claims," for one of the ships involved, these disputes were settled in time for the election of 1872.

THE 1872 ELECTION. In the 1872 election, Grant ran as "The Galena Tanner" with his new running mate, Henry Wilson, who was known as "The Natick (Massachusetts) Shoemaker." Vice President Colfax was dropped because he was the target of claims arising from the Crédit Mobilier affair. This scandal involved the misuse of money set aside for the building of the transcontinental railroad, which had been completed in 1869. Grant faced opposition from a combined force of Democrats and breakaway Republicans but was able to win reelection. He defeated the Liberal Republican and Democrat candidate, Horace Greeley, the "Sage of Chappaqua," with a popular vote of 55.6 percent. Greeley died before the Electoral College met.

In 1873, a financial crisis occurred that led to a six-year depression in the United States. Grant insisted on issuing currency ("greenbacks") only if it were backed by gold. This did little to help his working-class supporters, who believed that the economy could be improved by a larger supply of greenbacks. This continuing economic debate would lead to the formation of a third party, the Greenback Party, by 1875.

The biggest scandal of Grant's administration, the "Whiskey Ring," came during his second term. The corruption involved the evasion by manufacturers and distributors of payment of taxes on whiskey. The tax collectors accepted bribes and some of the charges of corruption pointed to Orville Babcock. Babcock was still an aide to Grant in the White House despite his earlier involvement in the Dominican Republic scandal. Disregarding the evidence, Grant insisted on supporting Babcock. Babcock ultimately resigned his White House post.

Then, in 1876, Secretary of War William Belknap was forced to resign in the wake of a scandal relating to the sale of a permit to trade with Native Americans. This was a small example of the failure of Grant's peace policy toward the Native Americans. A more significant example was the inability of the army to stop those seeking gold from intruding on the treaty rights of the Sioux Indians in the Black Hills of the Dakota Territory.

In May 1870, President and Mrs. Grant held a reception at the White House for a delegation of Oglala Sioux. William S. McFeely, Grant's biographer, notes that President Grant had "a commitment to prevent the extermination of the Native Americans. This was the only issue, the only cause, mentioned in the speech (his first Inaugural Address) in which Grant had a deep and personal interest. . . ." (Courtesy Collection of Charles E. Smith.)

This intrusion led to an outbreak of hostilities that included the defeat of General George Armstrong Custer at the Battle of the Little Big Horn in 1876.

Grant was not nominated for a third term, but he did play a role in solving the election crisis that led to the victory of the Republican candidate, Rutherford B. Hayes. Grant's last State of the Union message to Congress, on 5 December 1876, acknowledged problems in his administration. He argued that they were largely due to the actions of subordinates and his own lack of political experience. It was an honest statement but a weak justification for a man who had been president for eight years.

THE LATER YEARS. Out of office, Grant and his family went on a world tour that began in May 1877 and lasted more than two years. Grant met with and was honored by leaders around the world, including Queen Victoria of England, Tsar Alexander II of Russia, and the Emperor and Empress of Japan. In addition to the high and mighty, close to 80,000 people turned out to greet Grant in September 1877 in Newcastle, England. They held signs saying, "Let us have Peace" and "Nothing like Leather," honoring Grant for his role in ending the Civil War and slavery and still associating him with the working class. Grant returned to the United States in 1879 and was a leading candidate for the Republican nomination at the June 1880 convention. However, the nomination and the presidency ultimately went to James A. Garfield.

Back in the world of private business, Grant failed yet again. His first failures were in business ventures in Mexico and in Central America. Another failure was more serious and involved a company in which his son, Ulysses Jr., was a partner. Other partners unlawfully used business assets to cover loans and then were unable to pay the loans when they came due. The partnership went broke and at the age of 62 Grant was again a financial failure.

In early 1884, Grant was found to have throat cancer. He had been asked to write some magazine articles on the Civil War and, with the encour-

Mathew Brady took this photograph of President Grant in his Washington Gallery about two years after Grant's inauguration. (Courtesy Library of Congress.)

agement of Mark Twain (Samuel L. Clemens), went on to write his memoirs. Despite his often painful illness, Grant wrote two volumes that were eventually published as the *Personal Memoirs of U.S. Grant*. The books achieved both financial and literary success. They provided Mrs. Grant with a substantial income for the remaining 17 years of her life. Ulysses S. Grant worked up to the end, dying on 23 July 1885.

Grant suffered many defeats in private business, succeeding only at the end of his life by writing his memoirs. He also suffered many failures in the political world, where he placed his trust in untrustworthy associates. Often, as president, he failed to show the strong leadership he had displayed during the Civil War. As a later president, Woodrow Wilson, said of Grant: "He combined great gifts with great mediocrity."

VICE PRESIDENT

Schuyler Colfax
(1823–1885)

CHRONOLOGICAL EVENTS

1823	Born, New York, New York, 23 March
1854	Elected to U.S. House of Representatives
1863	Elected Speaker of the House
1868	Elected vice president
1885	Died, Mankato, Minnesota, 13 January

BIOGRAPHY

Named for the Revolutionary War general Philip Schuyler, Schuyler Colfax was born in New York, shortly after his father's death. When his mother remarried, the family moved to Indiana. There Colfax worked in his stepfather's store. At age 16, he began contributing articles to the *New York Tribune*. When he was 19, Indiana Whigs hired Colfax to edit a party paper to promote their candidates as well as their economic and social reforms. Later he purchased the paper and renamed it the *St. Joseph Valley Register*.

Colfax was defeated when he ran for Congress

as a Whig. Opposed to slavery, he was driven by his dismay over the Kansas-Nebraska Act to join for a brief time the American (Know-Nothing) Party. However, he won election to the U.S. House of Representatives as a Republican. In Congress, the good-natured Colfax gained the nickname "Smiler." Rising rapidly through party ranks, he was elected Speaker of the House in 1863.

Speaker Colfax steered cleverly between the Radical Republicans in Congress and the more moderate administration of President Abraham Lincoln. Although Lincoln suspected Colfax of being an "intriguer" and not completely trustworthy, they maintained cordial relations. Colfax declined an invitation to accompany Lincoln to the theater on the night the President was assassinated.

Initially, Colfax supported President Andrew Johnson's policies for Reconstruction, as long as the federal government protected the rights of the freedmen. When Johnson vetoed the Freedman's Bureau bill, Colfax allied himself with the Radicals. Although he considered his job as Speaker of the House more important than the vice presidency, he agreed to run with Ulysses S. Grant in 1868. A temperance advocate, Colfax countered Grant's reputation for hard drinking.

Shortly after the election, the 45-year-old widower married again. Two years later, in 1870, he became a father. That same year he made a surprise announcement that he planned to retire after his term. President Grant suggested that Colfax resign as vice president to become secretary of state, but he declined. Reversing himself in 1872, Colfax sought reelection but was defeated by Henry Wilson at the Republican convention. During the election, the Crédit Mobilier scandal tarred Colfax's reputation. He denied having accepted railroad stocks to influence his vote, but evidence suggested otherwise. Retiring to private life, Colfax built a well-paying career giving speeches about his wartime dealings with Lincoln. He died at a railroad station in Minnesota while on his way to deliver another lecture.

VICE PRESIDENT

Henry Wilson
(1812–1875)

CHRONOLOGICAL EVENTS

1812	Born, Farmington, New Hampshire, 16 February
1841	Elected to Massachusetts state legislature
1855	Elected to U.S. Senate
1872	Elected vice president
1875	Died, Washington, D.C., 22 November

BIOGRAPHY

Born Jeremiah Jones Colbath, Wilson rebelled against his family and legally changed his name to Henry Wilson. Apprenticed to a local farmer, he received almost no formal education and had to teach himself. When he finished his apprenticeship at age 21, he walked to Natick, Massachusetts, where he learned shoemaking. His business prospered, and he eventually owned a shoe factory.

Wealth freed Wilson for public affairs. He served in the state legislature as a Whig, campaigning as the self-made "Natick Cobbler." An outspoken opponent of slavery, Wilson quit the Whigs to run as the antislavery Free Soil Party candidate for Congress and for governor. Losing these races, Wilson joined the American (Know-Nothing) Party, whose platform was antislavery but also anti-immigrant and anti-Catholic. In 1854, he lost another race for governor, this time as a Republican. Soon afterward a coalition of Know-Nothings, Free Soilers, and Democrats elected Wilson to the U.S. Senate. His uncertain political loyalties earned him a reputation as an opportunist.

As a senator, Wilson stood firmly against slavery. When Republicans gained the majority in 1861, he chaired the Committee on Military Affairs. He also raised a volunteer infantry unit and briefly served as a colonel. Wilson sided with Radical Republicans who pressed President Abraham Lincoln to free the slaves. Later he hoped that Andrew Johnson would take a tough approach to the Reconstruction of the South and was outraged when Johnson vetoed the programs of the Radical Republicans. He cast his vote to remove Johnson as president, an effort that narrowly failed.

Wilson lost the Republican vice presidential nomination in 1868 to House Speaker Schuyler Colfax. His strong support for President Ulysses S. Grant led to his selection to replace Colfax for vice president when Grant ran for a second term in 1872. During the campaign, newspapers exposed the Credit Mobilier scandal, in which members of Congress — including both Colfax and Wilson — had been bribed with railroad stock. Wilson insisted that he had returned the stock.

Weakened by a long speaking tour during the campaign, Vice President Wilson suffered a stroke six months later. Poor health frequently kept him away from the Senate and prevented him from playing a part in Grant's administration. While recovering, he wrote a history of the Civil War. Wilson hoped to run for president himself in 1876 but fell ill again and died in the vice president's office at the Capitol.

THE CABINET

SECRETARY OF STATE
Elihu B. Washburne, 1869
Hamilton Fish, 1869, 1873

SECRETARY OF WAR
John A. Rawlins, 1869
William T. Sherman, 1869
William W. Belknap, 1869, 1873
Alphonso Taft, 1876
James D. Cameron, 1876

SECRETARY OF THE TREASURY
George S. Boutwell, 1869, 1873
William A. Richardson, 1873
Benjamin H. Bristow, 1874
Lot M. Morrill, 1876

POSTMASTER GENERAL
John A. J. Creswell, 1869, 1873
James W. Marshall, 1874
Marshall Jewell, 1874
James N. Tyner, 1876

ATTORNEY GENERAL[1]
Ebenezer R. Hoar, 1869
Amos T. Akerman, 1870
George H. Williams, 1871, 1873
Edwards Pierrepont, 1875
Alphonso Taft, 1876

SECRETARY OF THE NAVY
Adolph E. Borie, 1869
George M. Robeson, 1869, 1873

SECRETARY OF THE INTERIOR
Jacob D. Cox, 1869
Columbus Delano, 1870, 1873
Zachariah Chandler, 1875

1. Department of Justice established 22 June 1870.

(Courtesy Library of Congress.)

Hamilton Fish (1808–1893). Fish was appointed secretary of state by President Ulysses S. Grant in 1869. He had previously served in the U.S. Senate (1851–1857).

As secretary of state, Fish reorganized the State Department and used the merit system as a basis for promotion instead of patronage and favoritism. In 1871, Fish negotiated the Treaty of Washington, which settled the *Alabama* controversy (a Confederate warship that was constructed in a British port during the Civil War) and other matters of dispute between the United States and Great Britain. The arbitration panel awarded the United States $15.5 million in damages.

Fish was reappointed secretary of state by President Grant in 1873. He avoided war with Spain by persuading President Grant to remain neutral in Cuba's struggle for independence.

FAMILY

26 January 1826	Julia Boggs Dent born	4 July 1855	Daughter, Ellen (Nellie), born
22 August 1848	Julia Dent married Uysses S. Grant	6 February 1858	Son, Jesse Root, born
30 May 1850	Son, Frederick Dent, born	23 July 1885	Ulysses S. Grant died
22 July 1852	Son, Ulysses S. (Buck), born	14 December 1902	Julia Grant died

(Courtesy Library of Congress.)

Julia Dent met Grant through her brother who was Grant's classmate at West Point. They postponed their marriage for four years because of the Mexican War. Throughout his years of military service, she accompanied him as often as possible.

The Grants raised three sons and a daughter. The eldest, Fred, graduated from West Point but resigned 10 years later. He had a very interesting career. President Benjamin Harrison appointed him U.S. minister to Austria-Hungary. He followed Theodore Roosevelt as police commissioner of New York, and he was assistant secretary of war in President William McKinley's administration. He went back into the army when the Spanish-American War began, and he served in Cuba, Puerto Rico, and the Philippines.

Buck formed a brokerage firm, Grant and Ward, which his father later joined. The firm went bankrupt after a few years. Nellie married a wealthy Englishman in a lavish White House ceremony. The marriage broke up because of his drinking, and she returned to the United States with her three children. Jesse became an engineer and helped to develop present day Tijuana as a gambling resort. He sought the Democratic presidential nomination in 1908, but lost to William Jennings Bryan.

GRANT'S BIRTHPLACE STATE HISTORIC SITE

U.S. Route 52 and State Route 232 • Point Pleasant, Ohio 45153 • Tel: (513) 553-4911

Located approximately 27 miles east of Cincinnati at the intersection of Routes 232 and 52. Open April through October, Wednesday to Saturday, from 9:30 A.M. to 5 P.M.; Sunday from 12 P.M. to 5 P.M. Admission fee. Children ages 5 and under admitted free. Tours available. Handicapped accessible. For more information, write: The Ohio Historical Society, 1982 Velma Avenue, Columbus, OH 43211-2497. Operated by the Ohio Historical Society.

President Grant's Birthplace Cottage was exhibited throughout the country by train and later displayed at the Ohio State Fairgrounds. It was returned to Point Pleasant, Ohio in the 1930s. (Courtesy Ohio Historical Society.)

Ulysses S. Grant was born on 27 April 1822 in a one-room cottage near the Ohio River. It was built in 1817 and measures 16 feet by 19 feet. After Grant's birth his parents, Jesse and Hannah, moved to Georgetown, located approximately 20 miles east of Point Pleasant, where his father built a tannery.

The birthplace home has since been expanded to three rooms. The original room, located at the front, is furnished with antiques and period pieces.

110

U.S. GRANT HOME STATE HISTORIC SITE

511 Bouthillier Street • P.O. Box 333 • Galena, Illinois 61036 • Tel: (815) 777-0248

Located approximately 63 miles west of Rockford. Can be reached via U.S. 20 and Illinois 84. Open daily, March through October, from 9 A.M. to 5 P.M.; November through February from 8 A.M. to 4 P.M. Closed Thanksgiving, Christmas, New Year's Day; and on Martin Luther King, Jr., Veterans, and General Election days. Admission fee. Groups of 25 or more must have a reservation. Owned by the State of Illinois and managed by the Illinois Historic Preservation Agency.

On 16 June 1865, a small group of Galena citizens purchased the brick mansion on Bouthillier Street for $2,500. Two months later, they signed the deed over to General Grant as a gift from the residents of Galena.

(Courtesy Illinois Historic Preservation Agency; photographer: James D. Quick.)

On 18 August 1865, General Grant returned to Galena, Illinois and was greeted with a grand celebration. After the reception, a group of the town's residents presented Grant with a furnished brick mansion on Bouthillier Street as a gift to honor his Civil War achievements. It was designed by William Dennison and had been built in 1860 as a residence for City Clerk Alexander J. Jackson.

In September 1865, Grant and his family left for Washington, D.C., where he continued his duties as commanding general of the army. In the fall of 1868, the Grants returned to Galena and remained there throughout his successful presidential campaign. He made two final visits to Galena in 1879 and 1880. During this period, the house was maintained by caretakers and several improvements were made, including a new sidewalk and a spacious wash house.

In 1904, Grant's children gave the house to the city of Galena with the understanding that the site was to be kept as a memorial to their father. The maintenance of the site became too costly for the city. In 1931 it was deeded to the State of Illinois. In 1955, it was restored to its 1870s appearance. The house was rededicated two years later, which marked the 135th anniversary of Grant's birth.

GRANT COTTAGE STATE HISTORIC SITE

Mount McGregor • Wilton, New York 12866 • Tel: (518) 587-8277

Located off Route 9 on the grounds of the Mount McGregor Correctional Facility, approximately 10 miles north of Saratoga Springs. Must stop at access post for directions to the cottage. Open Memorial Day weekend through Labor Day, Wednesday to Sunday from 10 A.M. to 4 P.M.; Labor Day through Columbus Day, Saturday and Sunday, from 10 A.M. to 4 P.M. Admission fee, with discounts available for groups of 10 or more. Children ages 4 and under admitted free. Advance group reservations required. Tours available. Special events include a ceremony commemorating Grant's arrival at the cottage (June 16) and a memorial service marking the anniversary of his death (July 23). For more information, write: The Friends of the Ulysses S. Grant Cottage, Inc., P.O. Box 990, Saratoga Springs, NY 12866-0897. Operated by The Friends of the Ulysses S. Grant Cottage, Inc., in cooperation with the New York State Office of Parks, Recreation and Historic Preservation.

After Grant's death, the cottage was sealed by Joseph W. Drexel. As a result, the furnishings, decorations, and personal items remain as they were when he died. In 1890, the cottage was opened to the public. (Courtesy Library of Congress.)

In June 1884, Grant, heavily in debt from failed business ventures, decided to write his memoirs for publication. Later that year he was diagnosed with throat cancer. On 16 June 1885, he came to stay at the Drexel family cottage on Mount McGregor in Saratoga County, New York. He knew death was imminent, and for the next six weeks he raced against time to finish his memoirs. Mark Twain, his publisher, visited Grant in July to tell him that advance sales of his memoirs would assure royalties of at least $300,000 for Mrs. Grant and his family. On 23 July, four days after the memoirs were completed, he died.

GENERAL GRANT NATIONAL MEMORIAL

West 122nd Street and Riverside Drive • New York, New York 10027 • Tel: (212) 666-1640

Located on the grounds of Riverside Park overlooking the Hudson River. Open daily from 9 A.M. to 5 P.M. No admission fee. Limited parking. Call in advance for group visits. Administered by the National Park Service, U.S. Department of the Interior.

In 1885, immediately following General Grant's death, Mayor William Grace offered the family a burial site in New York with the assurance that Mrs. Grant could later be buried beside her husband. After the funeral on 8 August 1885, Grant's body was interred in a temporary brick vault in Riverside Park at 122nd Street.

The Grant Monument Association was formed in 1888, and a design competition was promptly held, but none of the entries were accepted. Two years later, a second competition was held, and the design by New York architect John Duncan was selected. In 1892, Horace Porter, a longtime associate of Grant's, became president of the association and managed to raise $350,000 in 90 days. Altogether, 90,000 people donated more than $600,000 to complete the monument.

On 27 April 1897, the monument was dedicated, and Grant's body was secretly transferred from the temporary vault to an eight-and-a-half-ton red granite sarcophagus in the mausoleum. Mrs. Grant was interred beside her husband in an identical sarcophagus after her death in 1902. The Grant Monument Association donated the monument to the American people in 1958. (Courtesy Eastern National Park and Monument Association.) ▼

▲ *The General Grant National Memorial, popularly known as Grant's Tomb, is one of the largest mausoleums in the world, measuring 150 feet in height.* (Courtesy Eastern National Park and Monument Association.)

Zachary Taylor

David R. Collins's *Zachary Taylor* (Garrett Educational Corp., 1989) is a good biography that emphasizes his life before his presidency, which lasted only 16 months. (For junior and senior high school.)

Zachary Taylor, Soldier in the White House by Holman Hamilton (Bobbs-Merrill, 1951) is a balanced look at his personal and his professional lives. It includes short, well-written portraits of his family. *Zachary Taylor* by Brainerd Dyer (Louisiana State University Press, 1946) is a well-done general biography that emphasizes his military activities. K. Jack Bauer's *Zachary Taylor, Soldier, Planter, Statesman of the Old Southwest* (Louisiana State University Press, 1985) is another highly readable biography of Taylor. (For high school and adult.)

Millard Fillmore

Kevin Law's *Millard Fillmore* (Garrett Educational Corp., 1990) is a good introductory biography of this unexpected president, who took office upon the death of Zachary Taylor. (For junior and senior high school.)

Millard Fillmore: Biography of a President by Robert J. Raybach (American Political Biography, 1992) is a well-done general biography of Fillmore. Benson L. Grayson's *The Unknown President* (University Press of America, 1981), a short, well-researched volume that deals only with his presidency. *The Presidencies of Zachary Taylor and Millard Fillmore* by Elbert B. Smith (University Press of Kansas, 1988), an excellent joint biography, provides a good analysis of the Compromise of 1850 and considers the direction in which Fillmore was taking the presidency. (For high school and adult.)

Franklin Pierce

Edwin P. Hoyt's *Franklin Pierce* (Abelard-Schuman, 1972) provides a good explanation of the problems that eventually led to the Civil War. *Franklin Pierce* by Fern G. Brown (Garrett Educational Corp., 1989) is a well-balanced introductory biography. (For junior and senior high school.)

Roy F. Nichols's *Franklin Pierce* (University of Pennsylvania Press, 1931) is a well-researched and well-written study. *The Presidency of Franklin Pierce* by Larry Gara (University Press of Kansas, 1991), a detailed and insightful work for the general readers, includes an excellent analysis of U.S. politics and foreign policy during the 1850s. (For high school and adult.)

James Buchanan

David R. Collins's *James Buchanan* (Garrett Educational Corp., 1990) is a good general biography. (For junior and senior high school.)

James Buchanan and the American Empire by Frederick M. Binder (Susquehanna University Press, 1994) is a highly informative biography that emphasizes Buchanan's early career in foreign relations as minister to Russia and to the Court of St. James's and as secretary of state. Philip S. Klein's *President James Buchanan* (Pennsylvania State University Press, 1962) is an excellent political biography. *The Presidency of James Buchanan* by Elbert B. Smith (University Press of Kansas, 1975) is a highly readable account of the conditions and events that led to the Civil War. It also provides a critical analysis of Buchanan's leadership during that crisis. (For high school and adult.)

Abraham Lincoln

Carl Sandberg's *Abe Lincoln Grows Up* (Harcourt Brace Jovanovich, 1956) is based on the first 27 chapters in Sandberg's classic biography. It is an excellent portrait of Lincoln as a boy growing into manhood. *The Apprenticeship of Abraham Lincoln* by Olivia Coolidge (Charles Scribner's Sons, 1974) is a well-developed introductory biography of Lincoln before he became president. Richard Kigel's *Frontier Years of Abe Lincoln* (Walker, 1986) is based on interviews with friends and family and provides a colorful portrait of the sixteenth president. *Lincoln, A Photobiography* by Russell Freedman (Clarion Books, 1987) provides an excellent photographic chronology of the events of his presidency. The narrative places the events in context. *The Lincoln Way* by Jeffrey B. Morris (Lerner, 1995) carefully examines both the events surrounding Lincoln's most important decisions and the effects of these decisions on history. (For junior and senior high school.)

Carl Sandberg's *Abraham Lincoln: The Prairie Years and the War Years* (Harcourt Brace Jovanovich, 1954) is the one-volume corrected and updated revision of his six-volume classic biography of Lincoln. Thomas H. Williams's *Lincoln and His Generals* (Greenwood, 1982), while not a true biography, offers the reader a great deal of insight into how Lincoln dealt with his Civil War generals and how he conducted the Civil War. *The Inner World of Abraham Lincoln* by Michael Burlingame (University of Illinois Press, 1994) is a psychobiography based on long-neglected newspaper and manuscript resources, especially those of people who knew Lincoln; it provides new insights into his personal and political life. *A. Lincoln: His Last 24 Hours* by W. Emerson Reck (McFarland, 1987) provides a detailed account of his last day. An appendix lists some of the still unanswered questions about the assassination. *Lincoln* by Philip B. Kunhardt Jr. (Knopf, 1992), the companion volume to a television documentary, is an excellent pictorial history, especially of Lincoln's presidency and the Civil War. *The Last Best Hope of Earth: Abraham Lincoln and the Promise of America* by Mark E. Neely Jr. (Harvard University Press, 1993) creates a vivid portrait of Lincoln based on extensive research into many minor aspects of his life. David H. Donald's *Lincoln* (Simon & Schuster, 1995) is an excellent, well-balanced biography that draws on the personal papers of Lincoln and his contemporaries. (For high school and adult.)

David R. Collins's *Shattered Dreams: The Story of Mary Todd Lincoln* (Morgan Reynolds, 1994) is a well-rounded introductory biography of a heavily criticized First Lady. (For junior high school.)

Mary Todd Lincoln: Her Life and Letters by Justin G. Turner (Knopf, 1972) presents her letters, spanning 42 years, along with additional historical and biographical material, to create an interesting portrait of the First Lady. *Mary Todd Lincoln* by Jean H. Baker (Norton, 1987) offers valuable insights into her actions as First Lady and during her widowhood. (For high school and adult.)

An excellent three-video cassette series is *Lincoln: Making of a President, Lincoln: Pivotal Year 1863,* and *Lincoln: Now He Belongs to the Ages* by David H. Donald (PBS Video, 1993). (For all ages.)

ANDREW JOHNSON

William Severn's *In Lincoln's Footsteps* (Ives Washburn, 1966) is a well-balanced introductory biography of Andrew Johnson. Cathy E. Dubowski's *Andrew Johnson: Rebuilding the Union* (Silver Burdett Press, 1991) emphasizes his life after he became president. (For junior high school.)

Andrew Johnson: Tailor from Tennessee by William D. Crane (Dodd, Mead, 1968) is a useful general biography with emphasis on his early years and personal life. (For junior and senior high school.)

High Crimes and Misdemeanors by Gene Smith (Morrow, 1977) is an excellent recounting of the actions of Andrew Johnson after he became president and the events in Congress that led to his impeachment. Hans L. Trefousse's *Andrew Johnson* (Norton, 1989) is a fine recounting of his early life as well as his political life after his term as president was over. *The Presidency of Andrew Johnson* by Albert Castel (Regents Press of Kansas, 1979) discusses his failures during Reconstruction and his impeachment trial in great detail. (For high school and adult.)

ULYSSES S. GRANT

Steven O'Brien's *Ulysses S. Grant* (Chelsea House, 1991) is an excellent, well-balanced introductory biography with some emphasis on the events of the Civil War. Another well-balanced biography is Henry Thomas's *Ulysses S. Grant* (G. P. Putnam's Sons, 1961). (For junior high school.)

Bruce Catton's *Grant Moves South* (Little, Brown, 1960) chronicles his military career and is especially good on the Civil War battles along the Mississippi River and on his growth as a general and as a leader of troops. *Lee and Grant: A Dual Biography* by Gene Smith (Promontory, 1984) traces the parallel lives of the two great generals of the Civil War. *Grant* by William S. McFeely (Norton, 1982) is a critical analysis of his performance as a general and provides some insight into the corruption of his presidency. (For high school and adult.)

Alice Fleming's *General's Lady* (J. B. Lippincott, 1971) is a well-written biography of Julia Grant that describes the Grants' army life in the nineteenth century. (For junior high school.)

The Personal Memoirs of Julia Dent Grant, edited by John Y. Simon (G. P. Putnam's Sons, 1975), provides a fascinating perspective on life in the army and on the presidency. (For high school and adult.)

at a glance . . .

President	Volume	President	Volume	President	Volume
George Washington	1	James Buchanan	3	Calvin Coolidge	5
John Adams	1	Abraham Lincoln	3	Herbert Hoover	5
Thomas Jefferson	1	Andrew Johnson	3	Franklin D. Roosevelt	6
James Madison	1	Ulysses S. Grant	3	Harry S. Truman	6
James Monroe	1	Rutherford B. Hayes	4	Dwight D. Eisenhower	6
John Quincy Adams	2	James A. Garfield	4	John F. Kennedy	6
Andrew Jackson	2	Chester A. Arthur	4	Lyndon B. Johnson	6
Martin Van Buren	2	Grover Cleveland	4	Richard M. Nixon	7
William Henry Harrison	2	Benjamin Harrison	4	Gerald R. Ford	7
John Tyler	2	William McKinley	4	Jimmy Carter	7
James K. Polk	2	Theodore Roosevelt	5	Ronald Reagan	7
Zachary Taylor	3	William Howard Taft	5	George Bush	7
Millard Fillmore	3	Woodrow Wilson	5	Bill Clinton	7
Franklin Pierce	3	Warren G. Harding	5		